FOOTBALL
CONFIDENTIAL

IAN BENT, RICHARD McILROY,
KEVIN MOUSLEY AND PETER WALSH

First published 2000
© Ian Bent, Richard McIlroy, Kevin Mousley and Peter Walsh 1999
The moral right of the authors has been asserted

ISBN 0 563 55149 6

Published by BBC Worldwide Limited,
Woodlands, 80 Wood Lane, London W12 0TT

Commissioning Editor: Ben Dunn
Project Editor: Barnaby Harsent
Designer: Linda Blakemore
Cover Artwork: Peacock design

Printed and bound in Great Britain by Mackays of Chatham
Cover printed by Belmont Press Limited, Northampton

CONTENTS

FOREWORD

The tears welled up and his face contorted in childlike anguish. Then Paul Gascoigne burst out crying, kissed his England shirt held in two clenched fists and football changed forever.

As symbolic moments go it stands as potent as any in sport. So potent that Gazza's tearful performance in the game against the Germans at Italia 90 transcended sporting interest and became a shared cultural event for the whole nation. Suddenly it was respectable for academics, high-brow novelists, agony aunts, sociologists, commentators of any conceivable hue and, of course, politicians to go slumming it in the working-man's game. Football was more than merely rehabilitated from the horrors of hooligans, Heysel and Hillsborough, it was fashionable.

Two years later, the transformation was complete when – after a bidding process as closely fought and enthralling as that fateful semi-final – the Premier League sold itself to Sky and the BBC for £305 million. At least in the top flight, with its spick-and-span post-*Taylor Report* stadia, fans flocked to the game; national newspapers sprouted extra sport sections; transfer fees reached unimaginable levels; clubs floated on the stock exchange, Brazilians signed for Middlesborough, and Manchester United became the richest club in the world.

Football was now not only the world's biggest sport but also the fastest-growing. Yet for all the attention of the world's media it remained a pretty secretive and unaccountable business. There were scandals and scams, rip-offs and bungs, corruption and crooks. There was also innocent but bumbling incompetence and rank stupidity. It was a business ripe for journalists to explore and expose.

Perfectly – indeed uniquely – placed to fulfil this task was *On The Line*. Launched on BBC 2 in 1989, it started life as a magazine programme with the regulation three items and a bit of chat presented by future broadcast stars like John Inverdale. Then in 1992, concurrent with the football revolution, it changed in character.

Former *World In Action* producer Vyv Simson took the helm and made it a hard-hitting, single-issue documentary series in the style of the long-running Granada programme. It certainly made its mark; two men filmed feeding live rabbits to greyhounds were jailed as a result and an outdoor pursuits centre was closed down following another investigation.

In October 1994 *On The Line* left television and was picked up by the recently launched Radio 5 Live. Its first programme was a prescient piece by Ian Bent called 'Along White Lines', highlighting a growing problem of recreational drug use among professional footballers. Three weeks later the Arsenal and England star Paul Merson confessed to his cocaine problem in the pages of a Sunday newspaper.

Since then there have been 14 series; more than 100 half-hour investigations into sports as diverse as boxing, bowls, basketball, martial arts, running, cycling, cricket, golf and rugby. But football has remained a mainstay; it is, after all, Britain's national sport. Millions of us play it, watch it and spend hours discussing it.

Some of the chapters that follow in *Football Confidential* tackle the game from the consumers' perspective. Why are local council pitches so dreadful and sometimes dangerous? Why will your kids never again get to play in competitive eleven-a-side football? Why is following your team around Europe such a drag and an expensive one at that?

All in all, *Football Confidential* is a journey through the underbelly of our national game covering the period when it transmuted from mere spectator sport into an entertainment industry. It is unlikely that if you sat down today to write a book on the nature of modern football from scratch that you would visit all the subject matter you can read here. Each piece stands alone and each reflects a different facet of the game. Taken together they are a revealing insight into football during the 1990s and the ideas and actions of the people who run it.

In a word we hope that this book is distinctive. Distinctive in the same way that the radio series has proved itself to be. The powers-that-be at Radio 5 Live have credited *On The Line* as being one of the unique selling points of the network. Because as good as the match commentaries, events coverage and phone-ins are – and Radio 5 Live's are the best – as genres they can be found elsewhere on a radio dial. An investigative documentary series is a different matter. It is expensive, takes time and involves risk. For having faith in us, we thank our commissioning editors.

•

Football, Pele's 'Beautiful Game', has many wonderful qualities. This book is not about them. It is an attempt to illuminate the darker side of the sport, to reveal some of the secrets that the authorities or those with vested interests would prefer you not to know. 'News is something that someone, somewhere, wants to suppress,' a great newspaper magnate once said. *Football Confidential* is our attempt to apply that dictum to soccer.

Ian Bent, Richard McIlroy, Kevin Mousley and Peter Walsh
August, 1999

CHAPTER ONE

A Law Unto Himself

The Lawyer Who Changed the Face of Football

It was not until a rather unremarkable Belgium footballer teamed up with an hitherto unremarkable young lawyer also from Belgium, that a remarkable change in the way football and ultimately all sport is run was made – all due to his girlfriend living a few doors down from the footballer's parents.

Take a walk in the thriving Brussels legal district, and head down one of the smart, fashionable but quiet streets, and you will come to the law office of the smart, fashionable but quiet Jean-Louis DuPont. Tall and slim in his early thirties, sporting trendy designer glasses, he has more the appearance of a town-planner than one of the most influential law brains on the Continent.

It is this man that the European Commission credits with the foresight and courage to change the way sport now operates.

Inside, his high-ceiling office is sparse, with a few modest cuttings and pictures illustrating the impact DuPont has made on the world of football. Opposite his large desk are shelves with football magazines from around the world, testament to the game's rise in popularity and profile over the past few years.

Although it is the name Bosman that is now as famous in world football as Pele's, Beckenbauer's and Maradona's, it is undoubtedly DuPont who was the the architect of the victory. DuPont, though, candidly admits that as a young lawyer, fresh out of university, his involvement in the case is no more than a lucky coincidence.

`I had mastered in European Law while my future wife was living a few doors down from Bosman's parents' house. And when Bosman had the problem, he decided rather than go to his parents' lawyer – he understood that it was something about European Law, a French club, and a Belgium club, and UEFA regulations – he knocked at my door, and we went to the law firm and looked at the problem.'

Despite the fact that Jean-Marc Bosman was no longer under contract with his former Belgian club, it took four years to finally settle 'the problem' with the Belgium football authorities, after the European Court of Justice agreed that it was illegal to prohibit him from moving to Dunkirk of France from his then club RC Liege of Belgium.

The logic of the case obviously appealed to the young lawyer, understandably keen to make an impact.

After an initial look at the facts he was confident the case was black and white, and there was no chance of the court finding any middle ground, as long as they tackled it from what he calls 'the European dimension'. DuPont admits that they were fully aware even at that early stage that their journey would end in some sort of football revolution.

'We tried for a couple of hours to make phone calls to settle the matter in a friendly way. But we are talking about Belgium at the beginning of the 1990s when sport was one world and law another, and the answer we got was "Who is that lawyer who thinks he can ring up our club?" These regulations are world regulations, what are you talking about?'

After a long and costly legal battle, on 15 December 1995, the transfer system in football was shattered by the European Courts of Justice, as Jean-Marc Bosman stepped out of the court-room victorious.

Technically the football authorities were in breach of Articles 48, 85 and 86 of the 1957 Treaty of Rome. Simply: no worker is bound to an employer when a contract has ended, so why should he as a footballer be bound to a club when his contract has ended?

Many in England feared the implications. Some felt that the smaller clubs would be left to die as the bigger clubs spied their better players. Also there was to be a lifting of the quotas of overseas players so there would be a flood of cheaper foreign players into the game, not all of them an improvement on the homegrown talent already available.

So far the latter is certainly true, but what has also emerged is that the power in the game has now shifted from the board-room to the dressing-room. Players such as Liverpool's Steve McManaman, have used the new laws to engineer lucrative moves abroad, taking full advantage of the fact that the buying club has no fee to pay and the players' existing employers have no hold on them.

One of the first players to benefit from 'The Bosman Ruling' was Scotland's Paul Lambert. Once a reliable, but hardly spectacular midfielder with Motherwell, he was out of contract and went on a trial with Borrussia Dortmund in Germany, where he impressed the manager.

'Motherwell offered me a contract at the end of my three years which I didn't think was suitable for my family so, as I had nothing in Britain at all, I had to take the chance, and the next best thing was abroad. I had a week at PSV with Dick Advocaat and although that went very well, he said he wanted a wide-right player to take people on and that wasn't my game, so that was fair enough. I had another opportunity at Dortmund and after Dortmund if that hadn't worked out then I was coming back to Motherwell. Things went well at Dortmund and I was a very lucky person to get what I did.'

The move abroad certainly worked for Lambert. In his one season in the Bundesliga he was a European Cup winner after Dortmund beat Juventus in the final, and was well liked by the fans, who demanded a lap of honour from him after his last game.

Now one of the most respected midfielders in Britain, Lambert says he is grateful to Bosman for prizing open the gates for players like him.

'I went abroad and nobody had to pay a transfer fee and any money I was going to make was going to be my own, so from that point of view it was important for me and my family. I had a young son at that time, and had to look after them as well, so from that point of view the Bosman ruling was the best option for me.'

The gratitude of the numerous footballers across the world who benefited from his legal handiwork, as well as the sacrifices Bosman made to have a transfer technicality in football named after him, is all very well according to DuPont.

'It's nice to hear that there are people who are grateful because a lot of people multiplied their salaries by three or five times. If there is somebody to thank here it is Bosman, yet I can tell you that not one single footballer in Europe has made a financial gesture in his favour. If you gave me the right numbers of the lottery I would give you something in return, so that's surprising .'

In spring 1999 Bosman eventually received £350,000 from the Belgian Football Association. His football career is now over, and he plays a lot of tennis. Jean-Louis DuPont's reward is that he is now one of the most sought after sports lawyers in Europe.

DuPont's reputation stretched to the impressive European Council buildings a short walk from his chambers, where former Wimbledon tennis player Angela Billingham was an MEP at the time. As secretary of the EC's all-party sports group she was heavily involved in the Commissions sports policy, before losing her seat in the 1999 Euro elections. She fully recognizes the impact of the Bosman case.

'One commentator has described it as a release from slavery. I wouldn't put it quite like that but these people had been tied in a grossly unfair way and, as their advocate, he put their case superbly. The rest is history.'

The fact that the EC now has a group dedicated to sport, and with such influence, is again in part a result of DuPont's work. It's remarkable in itself that sport is now seen as a political issue, and will form a significant part of any future European Treaty.

Only time will tell what the structure of the treaty – and the role of sports in it – will be, but there is no doubt that the Bosman case has shown that the governing bodies of sport no longer rule with an almost 'Papal Infallibility' who never have their authority challenged.

In this country the recent case involving the Office of Fair Trading, and its failed challenge to the Premier League's television deal is a prime example. The question being: is sport a cultural and recreational activity that benefits millions of people, or a huge business generating millions of pounds and therefore subject to the same laws and business practices as any corporation?

The Bosman ruling places sport firmly in the latter category. But if sport, and football as its most lucrative concern, is to follow the letter of the law, as practised by Jean-Louis DuPont and the many other lawyers now beavering away in this area, much of what we know and take for granted will simply not have a place.

Years after they left Plough Lane, Wimbledon Football Club, having lodged unsatisfactorily at several grounds in London while trying to find permanent base, is still searching for a home to call its own. When the idea was mooted that the club may move from South London and relocate to Clondalkin on the outskirts Dublin while still keeping their Premiership place, it not surprisingly caused an outcry amongst the loyal 'Dons fans.

For Sam Hamman, the club's flamboyant Chairman, frustrated in his attempts to find a new home, the move made sense. His club needs a home and Dublin was offering one, plus a huge fan base built on the success of the Jack Charlton years. Most importantly, Dublin is the only capital city in Europe without a top-class team; the one thing that was missing was a big club that the Irish people could call their own.

The opposition from the Wimbledon fans who held up 'Dublin = Death' banners at home games, was matched by that of the Irish Football Authorities and UEFA, fearful of damage to the existing leagues. The task of navigating Wimbledon's passage across the Irish Sea fell to Jean-Louis DuPont.

The question for DuPont was as simple as when he took on the Bosman case. Do the Irish Football authorities have the power to stop a company trading within the country's borders? Again, just like his early meetings with Bosman, the implications fascinated him.

Sam Hamman has an incredible enthusiasm and when you see someone like that you feel like getting involved. But what is very interesting about the Wimbledon case is that it's a very simple one. On the one hand you have Wimbledon saying: I can move to Dublin, I can have my stadium there, my Premiership colleagues have agreed to play me there so I can do that. There is the Treaty of Rome and I am a company – I can move. On the other hand, you have the Irish federation saying: No, you're not just another company, this is about sport and we are in the territory of strictly sports issues, and there is a rule that says, here is Ireland and we have monopoly on that territory and we don't want you here.'

If Sam Hamman does get his way and Dublin is placed on the Premiership map then DuPont says he sees even more far-reaching implications for the game.

'My conviction is that if Wimbledon is found right it could open a new perspective for football which is not a European Super League that everyone mentions, but the fact that we would have redefinition of the European map in order to have a strong domestic football. Take a look at Dublin. The problem of Dublin is that because they don't have a real European Club they're out of the map. I'm sure that if you go to Ireland you will find fan clubs of Manchester United and Liverpool not Anderlecht. Why? Because culturally we are talking about the same football market. That's why it makes sense for a Dublin club to play with English clubs. We're talking here about taking a broad-view look at the map and realizing that when it comes to football the British Islands are a natural market and that it makes sense to have a British Islands league. Call it whatever.'

A somewhat frightening prospect for football, although not for DuPont, is that if he did want Real Madrid to take on Arsenal scheduled by television executives then he would doubtless find a way to do it.

'For me there is just one thing that is really scary in the future of football and that is hiding your head in the sand only to wake up in five years time with a permanent Super League where Arsenal, Liverpool and Manchester United play out of their domestic market. Personally, I think that is what really concerns football fans. If nothing is done we will end up with that kind of American way of life when it comes to European Football. So when there is an opportunity for a brainstorming on these issues, I think we should welcome it at this stage.'

The more realistic vision DuPont has for football is not as an extension of the current European Champions League, with its blue-chip sponsors and carefully scheduled and immovable ad breaks, but as a Benelux League involving the better clubs in the Low Countries, a Central European League or Scandinavian Championships. In July 1999 the Scottish FA were quick to dismiss the idea that Celtic and Rangers in Scotland may see their future outside their domestic league and look to joining an English competition, but the 'Old Firm' will watch this especially closely. Although a puzzling notion to many, to the man whose vision of football is based on the make-up of European law, it is very simple.

From a plush office based in a rather unattractive part of Brussels' legislative area, Karel Van Miert once presided over the European Commissions Competitions policy. He left in 1999 to take up an academic post in the Netherlands. His term in office saw him take on many of the world's biggest companies which, according to European Law, were acting unfairly. It also coincided with the rise in the profile of sport and the EC's interest in it.

Before DuPont's missionary zeal he had little or no involvement in sport, but that then changed so much that he had dozens of cases awaiting his attention at any one time. It was his job to make sure that big business acted fairly and in his view professional sport was now big business. Mr Van Miert's position as Competitions Commissioner has been called the most powerful in Europe as well as possibly the busiest.

'In the first instance the European Union became a reality with specific rules and a specific law system and rules which needed to be enforced concerning free circulation of people, including sportsman and sportswomen, freedom of establishment, freedom of service and so on. So that's one side of the changed circumstances; on the other hand, the fact that professional sports became so commercial, so business like, meant that there was no way to escape the competition rules.'

Van Miert says he recognized early on the work of the new breed of lawyers, especially DuPont, who spotted dozens of glaring anomalies in the way that sport operates.

'Before the Bosman judgment there were only a few lawyers who were interested in trying to change things and bring cases before the institutions including the Commission, and Mr DuPont was one of the most active and most dedicated ones in this area. But then it was revolutionary work – outside the accepted structures, outside the sports world and mixed up with politicians and political life. Nowadays it's different because a lot of lawyers now think they can file any complaint to the Commission and get away with it.'

Angela Billingham, a member of the EC's cross-party sports group at the time of the Bosman case, shares Mr Van Miert's appreciation of Jean-Louis DuPont and his work

'I think he was a very special sort of lawyer – a lawyer with great clarity of thought – and a very persuasive, powerful man. But he also had one good thing going for him: he had an absolutely solid and proper case to propose. When you have fairness, justice and right on your side, it's pretty easy to be impressive.'

It is clear that Mr DuPont, as the man who lit the fuse for many cases involving Brussels and sport, is held in high regard. And, according to Karel Van Miert, such a radical concept could only have been brought to light by a radical mind.

'In the first instance as a young lawyer who knew a lot about European and competition law, he had the courage to go for it where perhaps better paid, well-established lawyers would not have been interested. Given all the pressures involved, it needed a young, brilliant person with a lot of courage.'

The pressure that Van Miert, during his tenure, along with DuPont and other lawyers, put on sport has prompted some of the biggest names and organisations to fight back. Led by the International Olympic Committee, and including Formula One's Bernie Ecclestone, Athletics Primo Nebiolo and UEFA's Lennart Johansen, a group met in Lausanne 'to confer on areas of common interest with a view to seeking the best solutions to the problems raised'. It was so wary of how far DuPont's passion might lead, that it demanded that sport be excluded from European commercial regulations.

Such is the confidence the EC has, it has already investigated one of the Lausanne group, and one of the most powerful at that, Bernie Ecclestone. The man who controls motor racing was challenged about the broadcasting contract he holds which reportedly allows TV companies which do not show any other motor races a 33 per cent discount on the fee they pay for the rights to show Formula One, which they consider 'uncompetitive'.

According to the EC, DuPont himself took on Ecclestone on behalf of the fans of the Spa Francorchamps motor racing circuit in Belgium, after they complained that their race might be moved to China due to the rules on tobacco advertising.

For the administrators of sport who have long held power and influence without any interference, there is no doubt that this is a shock to the system. But, according to Karel Van Miert, it is the responsibility of the individual federations to change rather than the laws being altered to fit the needs of individuals such as Bernie Ecclestone.

'Professional sport has become big business. Football clubs are floated on the stock market, broadcasting rights are sold for amounts of money which could only be dreamt of fifteen years ago, and there is no way we can escape that. One of the reasons is that since everything is now so commercial, we get complaints not from people outside the sports world, but from people inside the sports world. In this business the interests are now such, that if a club or league or other involved company feels that it is being unfairly treated, it will go to a lawyer and file a complaint with the EC. It's not because we get up in the morning and decide to go after cases in the sports sector, it's just that they land on our table.'

One case of interest to the European Commission involves Royal Excelsior Mouscron, a small club on the French-Belgian border. In a case closely watched by Wimbledon, the Belgian first division club attempted to play a home UEFA Cup tie at a nearby stadium because its home ground was too small.

Although on the surface this doesn't seem to be problematic, the bigger stadium nearby was across the border in Lille in France, which despite the difference in nationalities includes the town of Mouscron as one of its suburbs. UEFA laws do not allow clubs to play home games in other countries. The man called on to take up the case of the minnows against UEFA, with the hope he could cause a giant killing, was Jean Louis DuPont.

After playing Cypriot club Limasol in the first round, Mouscron was drawn against the French team Metz, and the club decided it needed more seats to match the interest of fans. To this end, it played the game at the 'Stadium Nord' in Lille, 12 miles over the border.

The people of Lille used the reasoning behind the Bosman case to argue that football is an economic activity and therefore UEFA should abide by EC law, which the town said it was breaking on two counts. Firstly, that it was abusing its dominant position in the market, and secondly illegally interfering in the right of one enterprise to offer a service to a fellow member of the Community.

The portly and friendly Jean-Pierre Detremerrie can justifiably call himself Monsieur Mouscron. He is the town's Mayor, MP and Chairman of the Football club. According to Mr Detremerrie, when they were looking to fight UEFA's decision, DuPont was the obvious choice to represent them, and in his opinion, the benefits were mutually attractive. He explained his club's position on a snow-covered night in a hotel in Mouscron's twin town – Rochdale.

'Of course, we knew him because of Bosman. He came and asked the people of Lille to fight against UEFA because for him as a lawyer it was a good thing. It was a case of, if he could win a second time against UEFA, it would be good publicity for him and good for his business.'

It is hard to imagine that the modest, quiet Jean-Louis DuPont would ever blatantly court publicity, but there could have been some appeal in taking what is essentially a small, local dispute and using it to take on the might of European Football's governing body, with the possibility that the case could turn football on its head, just as the Jean-Marc Bosman case had done.

'What was very appealing was that it's not about the club claiming it lost money or the chance of qualification. It's about two public bodies, the city of Lille and the city of Mouscron, that considered they had to fight a legal battle in order to make it clear that they are just one economic and social region, and that they couldn't accept a ruling from a sport governing body that would re-introduce a border that they had been working so hard for years to make disappear. So it's interesting that after one player – Bosman – public bodies were ready to challenge the rulings of governing bodies, when those decisions were not right.'

The repercussions of the case involving Mouscron will be watched by many in sport who are fearful of Jean-Louis DuPont's activities. Paradoxically though, he sees that the implications could be good for football.

'The Mouscron–Lille case is very interesting one for UEFA because I am sure that for the first time the EC will have the opportunity to recognize that some of the UEFA rules, even if they have economic consequences against the Treaty of Rome, can be deemed legal.'

He feels it is vital that UEFA, in arguing this case, do so with the commissions laws very much in mind.

'If you want to play football, want to take part in European competitions, you need a stadium, and the basic rule is that you have to play in your stadium. And that rule as such violates European Law in that you could say "No, I will play where I want". But because it is about football – because you need an identification between the club, the players and a region – I am sure the commission will deem the UEFA rule that says you have to play in your stadium, legal. Now there is an exception to that rule and it's a logical exception. This is that, if for a good reason you can't play in your own stadium, you can play in another stadium. UEFA, however, says you have to play in another stadium within your country, and that's where the violation of European Law comes in.

DuPont denies that he is driven by a personal vendetta against UEFA, but admits that he enjoys the worldwide recognition that he gets for winning the Bosman case – and one of the mementoes on his office wall is a picture of himself with Pele. In fact, far from wanting to crush the governing bodies of sport, he says that UEFA and the other governing bodies are necessary.

'The football world is not going to be nicer if it is only ruled by club owners and top TV moguls, and that's why I am very happy that UEFA is there. But I am sure that UEFA has to evolve, to have not a revolution but a dramatic adjustment to new times, and I really hope that it will manage that soon and in the best possible way.'

It is difficult to imagine a facet of off-the-pitch sport that lawyers or politicians, spurred on by the Bosman case, will not wish to involve themselves in. The ticketing policy of the World Cup Finals in 1998 led Karel Van Miert to accuse the French organizers of being 'anti-competitive'. In his opinion, tickets were not made available to all member states, and forced a climb-down. British MEPs took up the case of British ski-instructors who felt they were being unfairly treated in French resorts; BSkyB's attempt to buy Manchester United was thwarted by the Monopoly and Mergers Commission after much political lobby-ing, because that, too, was seen as uncompetitive.

The whole issue of TV rights in Football and Formula 1, for example, is one area where broadcasters can expect interference. According to Commissioner Van Miert, multi-year deals, such as the last two involving the FA Premier League and BSkyB, would now be illegal due to the advances in technology. In the future, shorter one-year contracts will be the norm.

Karel Van Miert can now look over the Commission from a distance, but admits that over half of the complaints that found their way to his office were football related with many of those hoping for a ruling to match Bosman. Since that historic 1995 judgment the knock-on effect has been such that the ruling has been extended. Players from outside the EC are now subject to the same laws and, if the EC has its way, the transfer system could be scrapped all together to allow footballers to move jobs and clubs, when, and if they like, just as thousands of other European workers do every day. Again the issue started in Belgium where the country's FA tried to stop players simply walking away from clubs by imposing a new type of transfer agreement. This was quickly deemed illegal by the EC.

The intervention and interference of the Brussels bureaucrats in sport looks set to continue. Before leaving office, Van Miert asked the world-governing body, FIFA, to explain its powers and criticized it for being undemocratic.

It is though, not just the governing bodies of world sport who have come under Jean Louis Dupont's legal microscope. Spain's main provences could compete on the world sporting stage under their own flags. The Catalonian regional parliament called Dupont in after passing a bill allowing the region's teams and individuals to represent them rather than Spain. It could pave the way for the Basque and other regions to follow, meaning dozens of Spain's top sports stars would swap allegiances.

It seems that only now are sports bodies catching on to the power and influence coming from Brussels. In Karel Van Miert's opinion they will only have themselves to blame if they take their eyes off the ball.

'They were very reluctant to draw the conclusions from the existence of the European Union – for instance, about the free circulation of players, yet, on the other hand, continued to pretend that sport was so specific that it should be, for instance, kept out of the implementation of competition rules. They were to some extent above the common law. Even today it seems to be very difficult for the sports bodies and others concerned to accept that logic.'

It is by rapidly accepting that simple logic that Jean-Louis DuPont has successfully carved himself a niche as one of European law's brightest stars and one of the most sought after legal brains in sport. The harder the governing bodies of sport find it to accept the laws, the easier it is for him to challenge the long held status quo that has kept the governing bodies in power for decades. This notoriety, he says, means that he now has the chance to cherry-pick the best cases around the Continent.

Cases like, for instance, the farcical saga involving Arsenal striker Nicholas Anelka. In the summer of 1999, after an unhappy spell at Highbury, he turned to DuPont to release him from his contract. Putting the theory in to practice, DuPont pronounced, to general amazement in the football world, that with a £900,000 'compensation' payment, Anelka could wipe his tears and be on his way. Again his theory is based on the rules that govern thousands of EC workers, who every day hand in their notices to employers. This is as blindingly simple to him as it is seemingly confusing to sport.

'I am happy that it gives me the opportunity to take nice cases where I can really show some imagination,' he says, 'not just reproduce something – that's the great thing. Logically, I have people coming from the major European sport which is football, but 95 per cent of cases are now coming from sports like Basketball and Volleyball. Then, all of a sudden, Formula One fans want their claims heard, or trampolinists, or people that come from a more discreet area. Obviously it's always easier to solve problems when you are talking about a small sportsman in a small sport, because European law is about economy and the basis of European law is talk about economic criteria.'

The track record that Jean-Louis DuPont brings from the Bosman case suggests that many of his ideas will come to fruition: teams will soon play in a Benelux or Scandinavian League; clubs will relocate American style to take advantage of an untapped market; and if an area can provide a service to a football club then this will be allowed.

In the next few years DuPont says he foresees half a dozen landmark cases, which will at last help to bring about what he calls 'a sense of balance' to European Sport. All achieved in a simple way with a simple mix of sport with European law and economic logic.

CHAPTER TWO

Star Wars

The Premier League's Battle With the 'Satellite Pirates'

It was the money from satellite TV that turned English football from a cheap-and-cheerful ferry service into a no-expense-spared luxury liner. There's something wonderfully ironic, then, that the single biggest irritant to that vessel came from modern-day pirates – space-age swashbucklers who scour the sky for opportunities to intercept football coverage and beam it into the smoky public bars of thousands of grateful pub landlords.

Watching football in the pub was a habit that Sky TV was keen to encourage, that's why Monday night matches were developed. But it was not allowed to show us games on a Saturday afternoon in case that stopped us going to the matches.

UEFA rules forbid a country from showing live matches on TV on Saturday afternoon. As the Premier League's then Chief Executive Rick Parry explained: 'That's a fundamental position of UEFA. We're bound by their rules that we can't transmit on Saturday, and there's always been a policy in this country that we don't televise matches in competition with live games – that means in competition with Premier League matches, football league matches or amateur matches.' So live matches can only be shown abroad where they don't clash with domestic football. That's why we can get Italian football live on Sundays.

Of course some matches are broadcast live in competition with other games – mid-week televised games, for example, nearly always clash with some amateur fixtures and often with the football league programme. And live Saturday afternoon transmissions to the Republic of Ireland can do little, in the shadow of such an attractive and overpowering neighbour, to promote the growth of domestic leagues. The Premiership, however, chose not to mention these facts when opposing the satellite pirates.

Sky and Mr Parry certainly never envisaged thousands of soccer fans spending their Saturday afternoons in the pub watching top Premiership action beamed in from Norway. But for the first five years of the new league, that is exactly what happened, and the authorities were powerless to stop it.

Tucked into the corner of a road junction on the northern side of Manchester is The Radclyffe Arms, a large, square, detached pub with a number of different sized rooms. In 1992 it was taken over by an enterprising young landlord, Lee Ashworth: 'It's a mixed sort of pub really,' he explained as he sat in his private lounge above the main bar. 'We have a good local trade and a decent night-time trade with a different sort of event on every night of the week. We have quizzes and karaoke during the week and at the weekend there's a rugby and a football team.'

Apart from the obligatory post-match pint from the rugby players, Saturday was Lee's slowest day: 'Down the road there's another pub with a bookmakers opposite and they got all the local trade on Saturday. We were lucky if we got more than a dozen people in during the day.'

Then The Radclyffe Arms climbed aboard an increasingly popular Saturday bandwagon – live Premiership football via Norway. Mr Ashworth says business varies depending on which match is being televised, but takings have soared: 'We'll take between five and six hundred pounds over the bar during a game usually, but if (Manchester) United are on then it could be as much as twelve hundred. It's certainly a big improvement.'

The Radclyffe's system was put in by Graham James, a local satellite whizz-kid with dark brown hair, pale skin and a taste in polo neck shirts worn under V-neck jumpers. He's one of a number of entrepreneurs who have made money by selling intercepting equipment to pubs: 'What we do is, we start off with places that have already got an existing satellite system for Sky,' he says, explaining the complicated procedure. 'We add on to that an eighty-centimetre dish pointing at one-degree west with a low-noise block converter, which is the thing that actually picks up the signal. We then give the landlord an A & B switch, so that he can move between the A setting which is Sky and the B setting which is the Norwegian Satellite. Then there's a D2Mac decoder which has to be fitted because the Norwegians use a different encryption system to the UK. The final thing they need is a smart card, which I provide for them.'

James reckons he's set at least 150 pubs up with Saturday afternoon football, in places all the way from Devon to Scotland. Lee Ashcroft says it was one of his better business decisions: 'It cost me £550 to put it in, but we made this back in the first week because the first game was Manchester United against Chelsea.' Like all but a small number of pubs, there's no admission charge, but the amount of beer drunk is formidable.

The day *On The Line* visited The Radclyffe, it was heaving. Punters had been ringing up or visiting the pub during the week to check which match was to be shown. Lee himself had called the answerphone of Graham James on Tuesday to check which English game the Norwegian soccer fans were being treated to. It was Manchester United against Everton, a guaranteed thousand pounds in the till.

The pub starts to fill up around one o'clock as fans arrive early to get the seats nearest one of the three TVs showing the action. By two o'clock the place is full to overflowing; a sea of shoulder-to-shoulder customers filling every corner from bar to door. At around two-thirty, Lee disappears upstairs to switch the satellite system from A to B. The TVs flicker and twitch and settle on the Norwegian equivalent of *Grandstand*, the eager viewers making what sense they can of the commentators. The graphics are enough to explain the team news and, when possible, many of the pubs play Radio 5 Live's commentary alongside the pictures.

Pirate football on Saturdays has mushroomed into an open and widespread activity that pubs and punters advertise freely, but it started like a furtive after-hours drinking club in a small number of secret pubs. The lingering knowledge that there were authorities which disapproved only added to the appeal.

The first pubs to show the Norwegian TV pictures of live Saturday afternoon football were in Newcastle upon Tyne. News of the latest attraction spread around the Tyneside grapevine like news of free beer, and soon there were reporters from the local press, and the licensee trade papers. Everyone was puzzled. Some claimed that it was illegal to show live matches on a Saturday, others said it must be piracy to intercept pictures that you hadn't paid for. The fans just bought their drinks and settled down for afternoons in front of the TV with their fellow supporters. Occasionally they could get to see Newcastle United, which, given the demand for tickets to the matches, was a cherished rarity for many of them.

Forty miles down the coast, Jim Sugget, the jovial landlord of The Green Tree in Middlesborough, was watching developments as carefully as anyone: 'I thought it must be a bit iffy,' he said, 'so I thought I'd ring up a few people and ask some questions. A solicitor told me that anything you can get from a country that's not in the EEC you can use legally, that's what satellites are for.'

Acting quickly on the advice he'd been given, Jim contacted a satellite firm in nearby Stockton-on-Tees and was soon part of the Norwegian TV gravy train. As former president of the Federation of Licensed Victuallers Associations he kept abreast of trends in the trade and says that nowadays no pub can afford to be without football: 'Every pub now has a corner with a telly in, and it's only there to show football. If you didn't have it then your customers would go somewhere else on football nights. Once I got the system to show the live games on Saturdays I was inundated with calls from other publicans wanting to know where they could get it.'

Jim's pub is a modern building next to Middlesborough's bus station. He picks up passing trade for most matches, but when the local team are on TV he says the place is packed: 'When your home team is on it does increase your profit, especially if they're away from home'. The Green Tree was one of the first pubs to show football on Sky, paying extra subscriptions for the right to broadcast matches in public. But as the satellite company increased its subscription rates, Jim Suggett found it was eating up all his profits. The Norwegian alternative, where a one-off payment for the equipment was all that was required, solved his problem. Soon, he says, many other members of the Licensed Victuallers Associations caught on to the venture: 'Yes, lots of our members take the Norwegian television now, it gives them a Premier League match every week for a single payment'.

As word spread, it became evident that the satellite pirates were operating in a legal grey area, created when technology moves faster than the law. The Premiership was adamant that the interception of pictures from Norway was illegal. Chief Executive at the time, Rick Parry, was furious: 'At the end of the day it's counterfeiting. People are broadcasting a signal which they haven't paid for, and we're going to stop it'.

Norwegian TV's contract with the Premiership was worth nine million pounds over three years. It allowed them to broadcast live matches every Saturday when there wasn't a game in Norway. Since the Scandinavian season only overlaps with the English season by a couple of weeks, it meant matches on Norwegian television almost every week. 'The point in Norway is that we make matches available only when their season isn't operating,' explained Rick Parry. 'It's only because of the phasing of the seasons in Scandinavia that we can broadcast for the majority of our season. When their season starts, we stop.'

The Premiership needed to end the Saturday afternoon screenings because the pirates were taking all the exclusivity out of rights deals. How could they sell exclusive rights to a company like Sky if all and sundry could get the service from elsewhere?

The pirated pictures are the same as you see on 'Match of the Day'. Signals from the BBC cameras at the grounds are sent to the London headquarters of the television company TWI. From there the signal is encrypted by BT and sent to the Norwegian TV company which puts on a commentary, encrypts it again, sends the signal into orbit and down again to Norway where the geography of mountains and fjords makes it impossible for a terrestrial signal to reach people's homes. It's the final leg of the journey, from satellite to Norway, that can be received in the UK, if you have the right equipment.

Paul Harries of Satellite newsletter *TV Live* says Norwegian television is one of the most widely hacked services in the world: 'The Norsk TV2 channel which shows Premiership matches live is broadcast from the Intelsat 707 Satellite. That's a very high-powered system that covers most of western Europe and is easy to pick up in the UK and it uses an encryption system which has been hacked since 1992. In the UK we estimate that there are in the region of 250,000 smart cards and decoders which will pick up this channel'. The appeals, says Mr Harries, are manifold: 'The cards supply twenty-five different channels mainly aimed at Scandinavia. As well as the football they contain major English blockbuster films which are shown months before they are available over here'. The cards, which also carry pornographic channels, are advertised widely in Satellite magazines for as little as ten pounds. A highly marketable combination of soccer, cinema and sex.

In the early days of the venture many publicans harboured lingering doubts that what they were doing wasn't totally legal. But as time progressed and more pubs were showing the games, licensees grew in courage. Some started to advertise openly with dayglo posters screaming details of next Saturday's big match.

In Norway itself, the craze which was airing their programmes to a new and unexpected audience was met with bemusement. Some commentators even made reference on air to all their viewers in pubs across England. Bjorn Taarleson, Sports Editor on the Norsk TV2 channel that carried the matches in Scandinavia, says that although live TV soccer on Saturdays is a rare treat in England, it's part of the culture in his country: 'It's an institution in Norway to have British football on Saturday afternoons. For a large part of the Norwegian audience it's a weekly event. It started in 1969 with another national broadcaster and now we have the contract to show it. For us it's an important TV product. We spend a lot of money on it'.

Mr Taarlesen, who spends much of his time flitting between Oslo and London, says that when he first heard about pirated pictures being shown in English pubs he thought it was just a minor incident: 'Originally when I heard about this it was because I was sent newspaper cuttings from England, and we didn't really think of it as a big problem. We also thought that it could be easily stopped in England because it must be illegal, but for our part all we were doing was sending out our signal as set out in the contract.'

Although Mr Taarlesen didn't think the pirate problem was one for him to solve, the Premier League clearly thought it was. He was summoned to an emergency meeting in London and told in plain terms that he was in breach of his contract, which permitted him to show games only in Norway. Unless *he* stopped the pirates, he was told, he would not get the valuable contract again. 'But,' he protested, 'I've got a contract which says I'm allowed to televise this in Scandinavia, and the contract also indicates how I can transmit it. If some clever guys in England make use of the signal in an illegal way, is that my problem or is it a British problem?'

Clearly, Mr Taarlesen saw it as a British problem to be solved in Britain, but he was in an impossible situation. There were other companies who wanted his contract when it expired, and he knew that unless he managed to solve the Premier League's problem himself, then his chances of renewing the deal were gone. He felt bullied and trapped. If what was going on was illegal, why weren't the rights-holders in the UK – the Premier League – taking action?

What the football administrators had realized was that the pirates were streets ahead of the lawyers. So the only way to beat them was at their own game. The Premier League forced the Norwegians to enter a satellite space race, desperately trying to stay one step ahead of people like Graham James in Manchester who were wallowing in uncharted legal territory: 'As far as I am concerned, we're not breaking any laws whatsoever,' Mr James boasted. 'I've heard all the legal threats in the newspapers about this is going to happen to me and that is going to happen to me, but they're doing nothing. You've got to ask "why?"'

In truth, behind the bold assertions from the Premier League that this was piracy and illegal, some prominent lawyers were less than certain. Stephen Bate, a London-based barrister who specializes in satellite law, explains the issues at stake: 'You have to start from the basic principal in English law that unless something is specifically prohibited by criminal or civil law, then you are perfectly at liberty to do it'. In order to make a legal precedent someone would have to be successfully prosecuted, but who, and under what law?

Copyright law relies on determining who is 'the broadcaster' and in the area of satellite matches this was more complicated than ever. Was it the BBC who filmed the matches, or TWI who collected all the signals in London, BT who sent the pictures into orbit, the Norwegians who brought it back down, or the Premier League which controls the rights? If the lawyers couldn't decide who owned the pictures that were being stolen, then how could anyone bring a prosecution? And who would they prosecute? The Norwegians for breach of contract, the pubs for showing programmes they hadn't paid for, or the dealers who were supplying the cards?

The Premier League was in a pickle, its money-spinning international satellite deals on the verge of back firing. High-tech transmissions were being stolen by a small band of computer cowboys whose enterprise was being fuelled by a voracious appetite for pub football which the league itself had promoted.

Stephen Bate says there is another problem which lies in the fact that the service intercepted is clearly Norwegian – as shown by the fact that it has Norwegian commentary and adverts: 'A right was created under the copyright act which authorizes people who send encrypted transmission to make a charge for the decoding of those transmissions,' explained the barrister. 'But to the best of my knowledge, and I may be wrong here, there is no international convention for encrypted transmissions and so there's a very limited degree to which I believe that foreign transmissions emanated from abroad have any protection in this country'.

Unless the Premier League's lawyers could find a way of proving in law that there was a British signal being ripped off, it would be dangerous for the league to take legal action. It couldn't afford the risk of going to court and losing, since that would establish a law which would render worthless all its deals with foreign broadcasters. Why would a foreign broadcaster pay millions of pounds for a signal that could be taken for free? The Premier League sells rights to 150 different countries around the world, many of them taking matches live.

While the lawyers scratched their heads and the legal bills mounted, pressure was exerted on Bjorn Taarlesen to find someone within his TV station who had the knowledge to outwit the hackers. For a number of Saturday afternoons towards the end of the 1996-97 season, a farcical techno-war was waged between a TV engineer in the Oslo control centre of Norsk TV2 and a gaggle of computer buffs sitting in their English suburban homes.

As the now regular crowds of football fans gathered in the pubs on Saturday lunchtime, everything seemed normal. What they didn't realize was that some of the bars contained spies. The Premier League had sent its agents into some of the pubs to check what was happening. This undercover operation served two purposes: first, it helped them gather evidence for any future court cases it might bring against landlords; secondly, it was the only way the authorities had of finding out who was winning the space race.

Thirty seconds into the match, the valiant engineer in Oslo went to work. One quick code-changing operation plunged hundreds of pubs into confusion. The pictures disappeared from TV screens in England but Norwegian sets, where the decoders had self-updating smart cards, adjusted after a few seconds and continued with the game. The move had caught the pirates by surprise, since they had no way of knowing that the techno-war had started. All over England smug looking spies sloped quietly out of the pub to ring in their reports. One-nil to the Norwegian engineer. But this was only the first leg of what was to be long-running tie.

During the following week the computer buffs went to work. Self-updating cards were obtained, copied and distributed. Information was circulated via the Internet and over the phone. Frantic landlords were given optimistic assurances to pass on to their demanding customers. As three o'clock approached the tension, among landlords, drinkers and spies, was far greater than normal.

Sure enough, thirty seconds into the game the picture disappeared. Punters, who had been told what to expect, waited to see what would happen. Within a few seconds the picture returned as the ever smarter smartcards found the signal. Only those pubs that failed to get hold of the new software were left watching fuzz. One-all, and the spies departed to pass on the news of a significant setback.

The season was nearing its climax with Manchester United struggling to resist the challenge of Newcastle. The tussle in the skies was just as vigorous. Could the Norwegian engineer lose the hackers once more? Were the copied cards smart enough to keep up with the changes? If the pubs won, then would the Premier League carry out its threat not to renew the Norsk TV2 contract?

On the third Saturday, the Norwegian TV engineer had to put in overtime. Thirty seconds into the game he switched the codes. The screens in the pubs adapted to the new signal as quickly as those in Scandinavia. Almost as quickly, the news sped back to Oslo via the pub spies. Once again the engineer switched the codes, but after a short delay the coverage was restored. Three more switches also failed to shake the pirates off.

Two-one to the pirates, and that was the final score as the start of the Norwegian season brought an end to the broadcasting of Premiership football in the fjords and spared the authorities any further embarrassment. But a lesson had been learned, the hackers had the technology to decode all the systems being used, so the only way to beat them would be in court.

Throughout this period there was a notable lack of public comment from the major breweries who were selling gallons of extra beer because of a legally uncertain customer attraction. Landlords told of how they approached their breweries' legal departments and were informed that they should carry on taking the pictures until there was clear a legal ruling that they shouldn't. Some of the satellite dealers who supplied the decoders claimed that they were being paid by breweries, but they could provide no proof and the claims were strongly denied. Bass, who brew Carling lager and sponsor the Premier League, took the decoders out of their pubs and instructed their landlords not to broadcast the Norwegian service. Rumours persisted that one pub chain was even sending up-to-date codes to managers every Saturday morning via the computerised till system. Again, nothing was ever proved.

When Mr Taarlesen's nine million pound contract for Norsk TV2 to show Premier League matches expired, the deal for beaming the games to the eager Norwegian homes went to the French TV company Canal+. The change of arrangements made no difference at all to those watching the games in Britain. The signals continued to be hacked, diverted and piped onto pub televisions.

During the close season the Premier League went to the High Court and took out an order claiming that dealing in the decoders and smart cards was illegal. In itself this wasn't law, it could only become law if someone challenged it and the matter was proved in court, but it was a more than a useful tool with which to threaten some of the smaller dealers.

The order was served on a number of pirate operators telling them that unless they stopped immediately they would be sued. Many of the dealers didn't have the money to join a long and complex battle with costly legal fees. They gave up, keeping the money they had made. Other dealers protested that they were dong nothing wrong and tried to oppose the High Court Order, but found the costs were too great. Another group of dealers held two fingers up to the Premier League and dared it to go to court. The techno-war became a courtroom scrap.

The small firm which stood up strongest to the challenge of a legal argument was based in Birmingham. The owners of Vision On (Midlands) Limited were convinced that they had done nothing that could be proved to be wrong. They admitted they had distributed the decoders and smart cards enabling people to receive the pictures from Intelsat 707, but disputed that they had gone against any interpretation of complex copyright laws.

As the date drew closer for the hearing before Mr Justice Cobb at the High Courts of Justice Chancery Division, Alex Rote, a director of Vision On, was talking a solid game. He was confident of securing a victory for the small entrepreneur over the faceless might of big business. The Premier League remained quiet.

Then, at the very last minute, a letter from Mr Rote arrived at the court. It read: 'I apologize to the court for our non-attendance at this trial but the company has taken the decision that it can no longer defend this action and will take no further part in the proceedings. Vision On (Midlands) Limited has ceased to trade.' Mr Rote's U-turn remains a mystery, but it gave the Premier League's lawyers an open goal in which to slot home their most significant victory to date.

The Premier League's lawyers then began to explain how Mr Rote's company had been threatened with the High Court Order and had agreed to stop dealing in the cards and decoders in July 1998, but, as the court heard: 'In December 1998 the claimant's private investigators discovered that the defendants were advertising and selling smart cards suitable for watching Saturday football matches on the Norwegian channel'. The lawyers continued to explain that: 'These were not even genuine Norwegian smart cards diverted to an unauthorized purpose. They are pirate cards. They are "self-updating" , i.e. they are, in principle, inexhaustible.' The mighty lords of football unleashed their pack of legal hounds on Mr Rote. His unexplained capitulation gave the judge little option.

The judge ruled that Vision On should be restrained from dealing in the smart cards and decoders and that the Premier League could destroy any relevant equipment owned by the firm. It was the final victory that the football authorities had dreamed of. With this legal precedent behind them there would be nothing to stop them driving all the pirates out of business.

When August, 1999 arrived, the Premier League bosses had reason for renewed optimism. But, if their spies were dispatched to spend Saturday afternoon crawling round pubs, they'd have received depressing reports. Despite the judge's comments, adverts filled pub windows with the brazen promises of live matches. Even with confirmation that the law is on their side, the Premier League faces a long and expensive battle against hundreds of small-time pirates who are either oblivious to the ruling, or who choose to ignore it.

And worse is to come for the football clubs who expect to reap a bumper harvest from digital television which will allow even more football to be screened. The new technology also means that the signals will not need to be bounced off satellites, and so will bypass the hackers who intercept the pictures as they return from space. Digital TV is already operating in the USA, the pirates have already shown they can hack into it, and many of them are relaxing in the confident expectation that they will be able to do the same with football in the UK.

CHAPTER THREE

The Great Ticket Fiasco
The Great France 98 Ticket Rip-off

It should have been the moment when justice was finally done. The European Union declared – more than a year after the event – that it *was* going to fine the organizers of the France 98 World Cup. They had, after all, presided over one of the biggest ticketing fiascos of all time, helping to create a huge black market that left many without the seats they had paid for and causing the collapse of specialist travel firms all around the world.

Then came the announcement of the fine: £650. *Six hundred and fifty pounds* About the cost of a couple of black-market tickets for one of the more desirable games.

'Derisory,' said David Mellor, head of the UK's Football Task Force at the time. '£650 is what you get for speeding along a motorway.'

'Likely to invite ridicule,' said Tony Banks, the outspoken Minister for Sport. 'If football is an international family, it is vital that its premier competition is open to fans from countries throughout the world. France 98 got it wrong on that score.'

The French organizers could have been penalized up to ten per cent of the total ticket sales after EU competition chief Karel van Miert accused them of running a 'monopolistic' operation that resulted in 'gross-discrimination' against non-French fans. But the 1000-euro penalty – not so much a slap on the wrists as a slight look of disapproval – was kept deliberately light because it was the first time the Union had reviewed ticketing at a sports event and, said Van Miert, those in charge could not have foreseen the problems.

French President Jacques Chirac was unrepentant, accusing the EU of interfering in domestic affairs. Anyway, the organizing committee had been wound up after the World Cup final – so there was no one to pay the fine.

It was a fittingly farcical end to what should have been a celebration of all that was best in the game. The most serious consequence of the French ticketing policy was not that foreign fans couldn't get into games because they were full of Frenchmen, but that the allocation system created possibly the greatest black market in tickets ever seen at a sports event – and left thousands who had paid upfront locked out.

Rewind to June 1998. On a sunny morning at a resort village in the south of France, a group of angry football fans are holding a meeting. They have spent hard-earned money for a holiday based around the biggest event in sporting history and have just found out that their promised tickets do not exist. A hard-faced young 'rep' appears. No, he hasn't got their tickets. No, they won't get their money back. Voices are raised but to no avail. Some fans set off to the ground anyway in the hope of finding a tout who might sell at the right price.

It was a scene repeated all over France as the finals got underway. Yet for fans like Ersin Ramiz, it should have been the trip of a lifetime: 'I'd been dreaming about this. I was so excited, my friends were so excited. We were like ten-year-olds before we went.'

Ersin, from Tottenham, north London, had bought a package from a reputable operator, David Dryer Sports Tours Ltd. 'There were four of us and we all paid £1,055 each. That included five games – two in the first round and three in the second. We had to make our own way to the south of France. It was full-board at a Club Med, which was very nice, travel to and from the games, plus a World Cup picnic. It was a great deal but the main thing was, we were there to watch the football. We'd have slept on a bed of nails, really.'

Within a few hours of arriving at the resort however, Ersin and friends heard rumours that tickets were unavailable. 'We were getting a bit edgy but then our tickets all arrived for our first game, so that was fine. The problems arrived when we came back from the Scotland-Morocco game, at about one am, only to be greeted by a lot of discontented, ticketless fans who told us David Dryer and his representatives had left. We didn't really believe it at the time. It wasn't until the morning that the full horror unfolded.'

Of the five games he had paid to see, Ersin was to end up with a ticket for only one. 'We were gutted beyond belief...'

Many people had similar stories, not just from Britain but from Holland, Germany, Japan and Brazil. A financial disaster was beginning to unfold.

The allocation had been flawed from the start. FIFA had given responsibility for ticketing to the French organizers, the Comite Francais d'Organisation (CFO), which decided that 60 per cent of the total would be made available to French fans. Add to that the large number – variously estimated at between 14 and 20 per cent – reserved for corporate sponsors and the actual number of tickets allocated to other countries was very small.

Fans outside France had two legitimate ways to buy tickets: via their national soccer federation or through one of 17 authorized travel agencies. But there were nowhere near enough to go around and a black market flourished. In theory each ticket could only be used by the person whose name was printed on it; in reality, that mattered little, especially as many of the tickets that found their way into the underground were marked with the names of the sponsoring companies rather than individuals. Adverts from unauthorized dealers began to appeared in national newspapers and on the Internet.

'We were aware from Christmas 1997 onwards that there was a bewildering range of adverts for World Cup tickets,' says Paul Thomas of the Football Supporters' Association, which fights for the interests of fans. 'We had faxes coming through from America advertising World Cup tickets. Everyone was asking the same question: "Where are these tickets coming from?"'

On 18 February 1998, UEFA President Lennart Johansson wrote to FIFA General Secretary Sepp Blatter:

As always, the ticket distribution for the World Cup is a matter that is widely discussed. As chairman of the organizing committee, I feel obliged to take particular interest in the distribution policy. I should like to ask you to let me have a detailed and complete list of the distribution of these tickets as per today. Furthermore, I expect to be informed in writing on a weekly basis of the distribution of further contingents or any changes to previous allotments.

Months later, he was still waiting for an answer. In the meantime, Mr Blatter announced he would be running to replace Joao Havelange as president of FIFA.

By then, the European Union was also taking an interest. Under its free trade rules, all countries must treat EU customers equally. Soccer fans complained that the French were acting in a partisan way.

Graham Watson, the Liberal Democrat MEP for Somerset and North Devon, took up their cause. 'Supporters from just about every country in Europe who had previously managed to get tickets for the World Cup found they were being shut out this time. The French were effectively carving up the ticket sales so that at least six out of every ten tickets were going to French fans only. This was clearly an abuse of various items of European law and so I took it up in the European parliament. I think the French knew they were breaking the law but thought they could get away with it and were prepared to pay the fine.'

Mr Watson and 31 other Euro-MPs launched a court bid to prove the ticketing breached EU competition rules. They failed on a technicality. Their case did, however, spur the CFO into some action.

'The CFO wrote to some of the companies warning them that they should not advertise tickets because they weren't authorized agents,' says Paul Thomas. 'What we don't understand is why there was no legal action to follow that up and place an injunction or a block on people advertising tickets, because it was done very openly. Ordinary football fans desperate to get tickets were reading these adverts and thinking they must be official because they were in a national newspaper. But it's exactly the same as standing outside a ground touting tickets.'

Worse, in fact. At least touts sell tickets they actually have in their hands. The agents were selling tickets they had been merely been *promised* by various nefarious contacts.

One of the most shameless agencies was Great Portland Entertainments, based in Regent Street, central London. Van driver Jim Gibbs, 29, from Stoke-on-Trent, bought six tickets from GPE at £100 each for England's opening game against Tunisia – or so he thought.

'I got my receipts for the tickets within seven days, which I thought was fantastic. The next correspondence I got was after an article in the *News of the World* that uncovered a ticket scandal at Great Portland Entertainment.'

Naturally, Mr Gibbs was concerned. But he received a soothing fax from GPE boss David Spanton:

I would like to assure you that with regards to obtaining your World Cup tickets you have nothing to worry about. Your tickets will come from one of the sponsors or federations involved (Gillette, McDonalds, for example) and will not feature a French name. You are guaranteed entry into the stadium with this ticket.

With reference to the article in the 'News of the World' I would like to make it clear that a great part of this article was pure fabrication. We do not dispute the fact that we are currently in disagreement with Westminster Council (due to our pricing of tickets) but the article that appeared was full of inaccurate information. As we would not give them an interview they saw fit to publish what they liked.

I can guarantee that you will receive your tickets on June 1 at the very latest. Enjoy the tournament.

Kind regards
David Spanton

What was revealing about the fax was that it openly admitted that ticket brokers were being supplied by sponsors and federations. This was in clear breach of the rules laid down for ticket distribution. But with so many tickets going to sponsors, many of them American and with little interest in the game of soccer, there were bound to be bucketloads finding their way on to the market.

On May 28, a Channel Four *Dispatches* programme revealed that Great Portland was getting many of its tickets from Vincent Onana, president of the Cameroon Football Association. The game was up. Great Portland was raided by the Department of Trade and Industry and on June 4 a winding-up petition was presented to the High Court. It said that the company had been paid £2.4 million for 40,000 tickets but could supply only 'a small fraction' of that number; that the company was believed to have obtained 17,000 tickets despite not being one of the 17 official tour operators; that it had been charging up to £500 for a £25 ticket; and that anyone who did get their tickets from GPE faced being refused entry to stadiums (a hollow threat, as it turned out). The Official Receiver was appointed as provisional liquidator.

Jim Gibbs's tickets never arrived. 'After days and days of telephoning GPE they still assured me I'd get the tickets. I actually had David Spanton's mobile phone number and I spoke to him in France and he guaranteed me personally that I would get the tickets, up until about two days before I was due to depart for France. But I just gave up in the end. After spending a lot of money on travel and accommodation we just went to France and tried to get tickets from touts, which we did, but we had to pay another £100 each.'

Other casualties started to come in. Glasgow-based Kelvin Travel announced that it would not be able to supply 640 customers who had bought packages because it had been let down by its non-official suppliers.

Then, on the eve of the tournament, Vincent Onana was arrested as the Cameroon team left for France. His involvement would later have dire implications for his country's participation in international football.

June 10. The opening day of the tournament and the first game between the holders, Brazil, and Scotland, at St Denis, Paris.

'As soon as we arrived in Paris we were meeting Scottish fans who had been let down by ticket agencies,' says Paul

Thomas of the FSA. 'We found ourselves watching the game in the Moulin Rouge night-club with a large number of Scots who had found out on that day that the tickets they had paid several hundred pounds for hadn't been delivered. From then on we met a stream of English, Scottish and other nationalities who had lost tickets.'

The stream broke into a flood. More than 1,000 Brazilians arrived to find their pre-paid tickets did not exist. A Spanish travel agency responsible for buying them said it had been duped by an American firm that had taken its money and then failed to deliver. Touts outside the ground were asking for up to £1,500 for a £40 seat.

On the same day, the Japan Association of Travel Agents held an emergency meeting in Tokyo and announced that more than 20,000 Japanese fans were likely to find they had bought 'phantom' tickets. Many of these were corporate and the ensuing hunt for tickets from touts – as loss of face is abhorrent in Japanese culture – forced prices sky-high.

On June 12, FIFA announced investigations into two new cases of allegedly fraudulent sales, one involving an employee of its own marketing arm who 'apparently sold tickets he did not have', the other involving an unnamed South American football federation. FIFA's acting general-secretary, Michel Zen-Ruffinen, said, 'We believe that in South America there is certainly one association which has acted in this way.' A newspaper reported that around 25,000 German fans had been affected; a spokesman for the German football federation said it was 'an absolute disaster'.

On June 17, the general director of ISL France, a company part-owned by FIFA's sole marketing partner, ISL International, and two other men were arrested on suspicion of theft, fraud, corruption and abuse of trust. It concerned more than 30,000 non-existent World Cup tickets. The scandal emerged when a furious Belgian tour operator complained to FIFA about not receiving 15,600 tickets ordered through non-authorized sources including an 'external consultant' to ISL France.

On June 18, police announced they were investigating a

mysterious 'burglary' at the Paris office of American travel agent Prime Sport International, one of the 17 authorized ticket firms; almost 15,000 match tickets had allegedly been taken. PSI was already under investigation after a Madrid travel agency complained it had never received more than 1000 tickets bought from them. A few days later, the head of PSI was himself placed under formal investigation – one step short of being charged – for alleged fraud.

There was more. France Telecom said it was looking into a report that one of its workers leaked a phone number that allowed thousands of tickets to be bought unfairly; the number let callers avoid a huge backlog of calls and gain direct access to the switchboard. And in Lens, a volunteer for the CFO was arrested for allegedly selling about 50 premium tickets after fans in T-shirts were spotted in the VIP section at a game.

Many of the biggest losers were businesses which had bought corporate packages for staff and customers. The deals cost up to £2,299 including tickets for the final, catering, transport and five-star hotel accommodation. Among the clients stung were blue-chip names like IBM, Amstrad, Bovis, Ernst & Young and L'Oreal.

Amstrad, chaired by Tottenham Hotspur owner Alan Sugar, had paid £8,000 for ten ticket packages. 'We've been let down in the past but never halfway through a competition and never after being kept so in the dark,' said a company spokesman.

Sepp Blatter – who by now had succeeded Havelange as FIFA president – promised a major investigation into the whole affair. 'Black market sales, including those by national federations who sell off their surplus tickets, are something that shocks us,' he said. 'This whole World Cup ticketing operation must be reviewed for next time. We need to take action now.'

Yet in the excitement and hype the problems were temporarily forgotten. The world's media turned its attention to hooligans rioting in Marseilles and attacking policemen in Lens; to Michael Owen's dream goal and Beckham's sending off; to Ronaldo's state of mind and Zidane's searing form and the joy of a French win.

The reckoning came in those days and weeks that followed. Great Portland Entertainment was wound up in the High Court on 22 July with debts of around £2.4 million. Barrister Adrian Francis, appearing for the DTI, queried a recent payment of £418,450 made by the company to an account in the name of VIP (London). He said another payment of £742,000 was unaccounted for. There was a 'suspicion' that the payments 'have been used for illegitimate company purposes,' Mr Francis told the court. He added that the investigation had not been completed because of Spanton's refusal to co-operate.

The winding-up application was supported by two other ticket agencies, The Mall Corporate Events (liability £3.3 million) and International Championship Management (£1.5 million). Both went into voluntary liquidation after buying tickets from GPE which never arrived and then trying to buy on the black market to make up for it. Mr Registrar Buckley said he had 'no hesitation' in concluding that it was in the public interest to make a winding-up order against GPE. Liquidators were appointed to realize and distribute assets believe to be around £300,000.

Others joined a growing list of collapsed companies: Champion Cup Hospitality, David Dryer Sports Tours Ltd, FRT Management, Shaftesbury Tickets, Central Events, The Sporting Occasion. Their total liability was well over £3 million. Many had driven themselves under by buying from touts to try to give their customers promised tickets.

David Dryer Sports Tours Ltd– the company Ersin Ramiz had travelled with – was a reputable firm running exclusive package tours to big events. David Dryer, 62, has been in the business for around a third of a century, was a pioneer of football packages in the 1970s and has been an official agent for the Olympic Games. For France 98 he offered a basic package providing accommodation at Club Med holiday 'villages' with optional excursions to matches.

'Bookings went well and the directors had no reason to doubt that this would be a profitable venture,' wrote Mr Dryer in a subsequent report. 'However, in February 1998 there was a sudden cancellation in the region of £200,000 of bookings by Tumlare Corporation, an agent in Stockholm, representing customers mainly from Japan. This meant the company had over-committed itself to Club Med. Attempts were made to fill these vacancies by the company and although this was not possible the directors remained confident that the venture would still be profitable although the profits would not be as great.'

The real problem was to be tickets. Like others, Dryer had been promised 1,996 tickets by 'sources' he refuses to disclose. But a week before the tournament kicked off, he was told that only 600 would be available.

'What we hadn't banked on was the extreme popularity of France 98, the accessibility, the incredibly good infrastructure, the enormous number of people that flooded into France from countries that one didn't expect to send many people and, most of all, the exceptionally high-profile and the commercial world's involvement in soccer,' he says. 'The market went sky-high and everybody was buying. It was no longer a matter of obtaining a ticket for a football match; it was a commodity market. And it became like the Gold Rush.

'And therefore people who we had shaken hands with, people we'd exchanged correspondence with and in some cases even given a deposit, didn't let us down, but weren't able to meet the total demand.'

Which is one way of saying that he had bought tickets on a promise through unofficial channels and then could not deliver to his customers. Mr Dryer tried to make up the shortfall on the black market but failed to buy any seats for the opening game, instead paying £8000 to send 80 customers to the Moulin Rouge.

The situation deteriorated. One London customer, still so embarrassed about what happened that she hasn't told friends, had bought a package with her boyfriend for a three-day stay based around the Brazil-Norway game in Marseilles. Once at the holiday village, they heard rumours that tickets were not available. Then Mr Dryer arrived at the village.

'He didn't say much at all. Just shrugged his shoulders,

really,' she says. 'Quite a few people stopped him on his way across the village to address everyone and asked him if there was a problem. He had a bunch of tickets in his hand and he just kept shrugging his shoulders and saying, "If you bear with me I'll explain everything". Then it was established that there was a hit-list of people who had tickets and those who hadn't. We were the among the ones who hadn't.'

Mr Dryer was running out of cash. 'I was paying something like £300 for a football ticket to give to my client who had only paid £100. In the end we ran out of money and I lost a fortune.'

On 19 June he contacted a liquidator. Five days later, he ceased trading and made his staff – and himself – redundant.

'As I said to people at the creditors' meeting, I'm terribly, terribly sorry and I just wish I could do something about it.'

David Dryer was wiped out by his loss. But others, like Great Portland boss David Spanton, bounced straight back. Unbelievably – given that he had now been involved in four failed ticket companies – Spanton reappeared trading under the name London Ticket Brokers. There was nothing the law could do to stop him.

Despite the strong words of Sepp Blatter, FIFA's initial response was underwhelming. When interviewed by *On The Line* some weeks after the event, press officer Keith Cooper said, 'I don't think we're apportioning blame; that's not really the appropriate thing to do. I think it's more a question of identifying the errors and trying to find out how to correct them.

'The simple matter is that the policy of the ticket sales was laid down in February 1995 and having passed through various committees, went to the European Community in Brussels, who approved it. National associations and the media were then informed, and it was only when it was really worked out in terms of numbers that people began to complain about it.'

Cameroon became the scapegoats. After the arrest of Mr Onana for selling part of the his federation's ticket allocation, the country had disbanded its FA executive committee. FIFA demanded that it be reinstated but the government refused. FIFA then proposed a new 12-man committee, with eight members chosen by FIFA and four by the Cameroonian government. But when Joseph Owona, the Minister for Youth and Sports, sent FIFA a threatening letter because it refused to accept his nominee as committee chairman, FIFA pulled the plug. In January 1999, Cameroon was suspended from all international competitions indefinitely.

The action was not enough to protect FIFA president Sepp Blatter from criticism. Early in 1999 the investigative journalist David Yallop published a highly-inflammatory – and very enter-taining – book called *How They Stole the Game*. It had much to say about Blatter's alleged involvement in the ticketing process at France 98. Blatter took out an injunction against the book in Switzerland and demanded that certain 'incriminating' passages be removed.

'There are passages in the book that attack my personal and moral integrity as a man and president of FIFA, and that I cannot tolerate,' he said. 'I have nothing to do with tickets. I reject all the allegations made.'

The Swiss legal system is tortuous and because of this it will be a long time before a decision is made. You can however buy the book in England.

One positive outcome was that ticketing for the 2000 European Championships, hosted jointly by Belgium and the Netherlands, has now been established on a fairer system, partly because the organizers feared a sizeable fine. FIFA has also enlarged stadium-capacity requirements from 30,000 to 40,000 for World Cups from 2006, to accommodate more fans.

'We are now working on a completely different concept from the last time whereby the whole ticketing strategy is now controlled by FIFA and not the local organizing committee,' said David Will, a FIFA vice-president and chairman of the ticketing committee for 2002.

Whether it will be sufficient to contain the ticket touts who come to feast on major sporting events is another matter. According to David Dryer, who is in a position to know, when demand outstrips supply in a commodity market, there is very little anyone can do to regulate it: 'If the World Cup comes to

England in 2006, the same thing will happen, the same organizations will be involved, and there will be a lot of people in this country, instead of in France, who will make a lot of money.'

And a lot of people who will lose out.

CHAPTER FOUR

I Think It's His Hamstring, Boss
The Shocking State of Medical Care in Football

It is before dawn, deep into the football season and the lights are burning brightly at a private medical practice in London. Inside, as the rest of the world wakes up to the smell of coffee, the air hangs heavy with the odour of liniments, lotions and potions, while an expensive set of limbs are pored over and pummelled by an equally pricey practitioner.

An hour or so later with the commuter crush in full swing a furtive figure slips from the premises and into a well-heeled motor which soon joins the morning jams. The figure is a well-known professional footballer. But he's not hiding from the long lenses of the tabloid press, he has simply been to have treatment on an injury. He's paid to go private because he does not trust his own club physiotherapist. If his club found out he could be in serious trouble.

Since he signed as an apprentice his day-to-day medical care has been in the hands of a series of men who have only the barest of qualifications. As he got older and his body became worth millions, the same inexpert hands were his only recourse to recovery when injured, unless the club said otherwise. Despite the fact that he seemed to spend more time on the treatment table than the pitch, the club were happy for the 'magic sponge man' to persist, until one day coming to the end of his contract, not to mention his tether, he decided enough was enough. He needed help and had heard about a clinic that would oblige him.

An unlikely scenario? Sadly not. Ask Martin Haines. Today he runs a chartered physiotherapy practice in Leicestershire but he used to work at one of the 'early doors' clinics, one of the biggest and most respected in the business, the Bimal clinic in Hammersmith.

'There were perhaps a couple of dozen players a season and we were only one clinic. I am not talking about your run-of-the-mill player, I am talking Premier League players even internationals worth millions of pounds. It goes against the way you like to do things but at the end of the day, it is the management of a patient that is paramount.'

One of the first patients that Martin Haines treated in this way was the former Arsenal, West Ham and Coventry midfielder Stuart Robson.

Robson was a key member of the Arsenal team in the mid-1980s. Signed by Terry Neil he survived the change in managers from Don Howe to George Graham, who arrived for the beginning of the 1986-87 season. The Gunners had made a good start but injuries were piling up. Robson felt he was under pressure to play although he knew he was not fully fit.

'I had been out with a groin injury for the best part of four months, playing on and off, but I had this injury and all the physiotherapists said, "Oh, it's a groin injury". The club doctors kept putting injections into it.'

As it happened, during this period Arsenal changed their physiotherapist. There was a six-week gap between the old physiotherapist leaving and the new one (the present incumbent, Gary Lewin) arriving. During this period Martin Haines, was hired from the Bimal practice as cover.

'Stuart came in with a "groin strain" and I had a look at him. It was not a groin strain, it was clear he had the beginnings of an incipient hernia, which is a small tear in the groin. I explained this to him.'

Stuart Robson was impressed with Haines's diagnosis: 'He said, "Right! To get this right you need an operation and when you have had the operation then you need to do these exercises and we'll have you back playing within six weeks". What he was saying was clear and definite. Then he told the Arsenal manager at the time, George Graham.'

Haines got a shock: 'There was some dismay that I had

actually discussed this situation with the player, without prior discussion with the manager and indeed the other medical people in the team and indeed I was chastised for this.'

Robson, even more than ten years after the event, is flabbergasted by the memory of it all. 'Well, it is amazing isn't it? George Graham did not want me to know that I had a hernia injury. It seems obvious to me now that they did not want to do without me for six weeks and were prepared to take the risk of playing me with a hernia.'

Six weeks later, having broken down again, Robson went to the club doctor who decided that he did have a hernia problem after all and Robson had an operation for the complaint. Put on the spot about the incident, George Graham denied Haines and Robson's testimony explaining that he never interfered in medical matters.

But Robson's nightmares were only just beginning. Transferred to West Ham the following season, he enjoyed a successful first year before breaking down with injury again. The surgeon used by West Ham (he has since died) had a strong belief that many groin and hip problems could be sorted out by fusing the pubic bone. Even at the time this was something of an idiosyncratic view, and today it is thoroughly discredited. But Robson went under his knife. Not surprisingly his injury situation did not improve.

'I had been there a year and a half, the contract was up. The surgeon said, "I have done my lot", the physiotherapist (predecessor to the current club physiotherapist John Green) did not have the qualifications to treat me, so I was just drifting into oblivion.'

Robson decided to take matters into his own hands. Remembering the treatment he had received from Martin Haines he contacted the Bimal practice and spent £10,000 of his money on treatment. He made a full recovery. Robson claims that going outside killed off any slim chance he had of remaining at the club.

'At the end I was an embarrassment to them. I was trying everything I could possibly do to get fit and one of the other players who had got drunk the night before would turn up late for training and they would say, "Oh, that's so and so, but Robson he's a troublemaker because he wants to go and get treatment elsewhere".'

He was sold to Coventry City where he became club captain before a cruciate knee injury finished off his playing career for good. West Ham have denied that he was criticized for going outside the club. Whatever the truth, under manager Harry Redknapp and John Green, one of the club's three chartered physiotherapists, West Ham's medical policy has since been completely overhauled.

As professional football players go Stuart Robson was unusual. Well-educated and articulate, he knew how to stand up for himself but he says most footballers, particularly the younger ones, do not have the confidence or knowledge to counter whatever the physiotherapist or indeed the manager tells them. In football clubs it seems you are often denied the right of any NHS patient – that of demanding a second opinion.

The kind of injuries Stuart Robson suffered with were hardly rare. They were, in essence, the kind you would expect a footballer to pick from time to time. And when he went to physiotherapists who knew what they were doing, he was soon fixed and playing better than ever.

In a sport where players are collectively worth tens of millions of pounds it is mind boggling to learn that many would be better off limping down to their local hospital casualty department for treatment because – amazingly – the majority of club physiotherapists are only minimally trained and indeed until 1987 needed no qualifications at all to work at a football club.

For years the job of physiotherapist at football clubs was a kind of grace-and-favour position doled out by the manager. It could be bestowed on a mate or a club servant perceived to have been unlucky in his career. Or it may have been passed around the loyal backroom staff. Certainly at Liverpool all the members of the famous 'boot-room' turned their hands to massage and manipulation at one time or another.

•

Bill Shankly may have possessed one of the all-time great footballing brains but his grasp of medical matters left much to be desired. The great man had a simple attitude to injuries. He believed the best way to get a player back on the park was not to speak to him until he was fit. It was a principle which led to some bizarre encounters between manager and players, as former club captain Tommy Smith recalls.

'He did not like injuries and when I pulled a thigh muscle which was an eight-week job, I can remember lying on the treatment couch in the treatment room with Joe Fagan stood over me. Bill Shankly used to come in and always talk through a third party. He would go, "Hello, Joe, how is Tommy?' Now, I would be lying there six-feet away and Joe would say to me, "How are you Tommy?" I would say, "Not so bad, Joe, not so bad." "Ask him how his injury is, Joe." "How's your injury, Tommy?" "Not so bad, not so bad, boss." "When does he think he will be fit, Joe?" "A couple of weeks." "He says a couple of weeks, Shanks." And he would carry on like that until you were fit to play.'

If you think this kind of incident is ancient history then you would be wrong. Martin Haines, who in his time has worked at half-a-dozen clubs, says an injured player is generally treated like an outsider.

'As crazy as it sounds this still happens. When they are injured, players are ignored so that – well, I do not really know why. I am trying to think of a reason and I cannot think of one. If you are injured you do not get talked to and when you are playing you are one of the boys.'

Thirty miles from Anfield down the East Lancs road is 'The Cliff', Manchester United's training ground. Like most things at the club these days, its gym and rehabilitation suites are a cut above the rest. Nearly a decade ago, as the Old Trafford club planned for English and European domination, they spent upwards of £250,000 on health and fitness equipment – and it certainly shows. There are the kind of weights and training contraptions normally associated with up-market gyms, such as rowing and cycling machines, to the more exotic giant circus ball (to help improve balance). United have the lot.

They also had Dave Fevre. If you watch football on television, the chances are, even if you are not a Manchester United fan, you would recognize Dave. He usually sat on Alex Ferguson's left in the dugout. Smallish, military-trim build, short frizzy dark hair and moustache. For all the fancy equipment at the Cliff, Dave Fevre was their most important investment. (Fevre, who had a spell with the all conquering Wigan Rugby League side before joining United, has now left the treble winners to link up with Brian Kidd at Blackburn.)

Dave Fevre is a chartered physiotherapist, which means he has been on a three-year university-level course. This qualification earns him the right to use the letters MCSP after his name (Member of the Chartered Society of Physiotherapists). If you have not passed the degree course you cannot use the letters and, under pain of legal sanction, have no right to call yourself a chartered physiotherapist.

Unfortunately most of us do not know our physiotherapists from our chartered physiotherapists. The difference, however, can be chasmic. Physiotherapist is not a protected title. You or I could etch a brass plate with physiotherapist and start trading tomorrow. We could not, however, call ourselves a chartered physiotherapist. However, given the predilection of English speakers for shorthand titles both chartered physiotherapist and physiotherapist become 'physio', and football has taken advantage of this confusion for years.

By the late 1980s, the FA decided it was no longer acceptable to throw the magic sponge to any old soul, and made it compulsory for all physiotherapists in football to have at least passed the diploma course the FA had been sponsoring at the National Sports Centre in Lilleshall. The FA would have liked to have gone further, but clubs have long resented any attempt to be dictated to and have taken particular umbrage to the notion of introducing compulsory qualifications of any kind. Thus we are one of the few countries in the world where it is possible to manage a football team with no coaching qualification and where proper medical care may be denied to playing staff worth millions of pounds.

The FA is proud of its course and in the context of the pitifully few professional standards it has been able to introduce into English football, perhaps justifiably. But quite what is the value of the FA Physiotherapy Diploma? Not much according to West Ham's head physiotherapist John Green.

'There are a lot of well-meaning people working in football who are extremely keen to do their job. But the argument I would put forward is: Should football clubs be employing people who have only done a basic 14-day training course to look after their expensive players, when there are people available who have done a three- or four-year degree?'

Green is one of the fiercest critics of the FA course and through the organization, Chartered Physiotherapists in Football, is campaigning to make it compulsory for professional football clubs to employ chartered physiotherapists.

'If a member of the public gets injured, they get seen by a consultant, yet there are clubs within the country paying £20,000 a week to players, huge signing-on fees, and yet not employing chartered physiotherapists. So, in my opinion, those players are seeing people less capable of treating their injuries than people who would just turn up at a physiotherapy department in their local hospital.'

The Lilleshall course, of which Green is so scathing, is not a two-week affair but a two-year one. It is described as a 'distance learning' qualification which, in plain English, means it is a correspondence course. It involves modules to be completed at home and then, at the end of each year, students attend Lilleshall for a fortnight of residential study.

By contrast, on a chartered course at a university medical school students spend nearly 4,000 hours in lectures and tutorials of which nearly 1,000 hours involve clinical practice on patients. The FA offers no clinical practice on its diploma course.

John Green is no voice in the wilderness. The FA Diploma course was one reason for the break-up of one of the FA's first stabs to get ahead of the fitness game. It paid for and set up a unit of high-powered physiotherapists and sports scientists called The FA National Rehabilitation Centre in 1987. This is now called the

Human Performance Centre and is a Sport England venture. John Brewer is a senior figure in the organization.

'When the diploma course became compulsory it was expected that the chartered physiotherapists working in the FA Rehabilitation Centre would help out with the course. However, we were unhappy with the diploma because we firmly believed football clubs should – and could – easily employ properly qualified chartered physiotherapists and so we did not offer our services. It was the start of a worsening in relationships which ended with us severing our connection with the FA.'

Despite these set-backs the FA persisted with its diploma. Hundreds of former footballers have now qualified on the course and are caring for players at all levels of the four professional divisions.

You might suppose that chartered physiotherapists who do work in football are all employed in the upper echelons of the sport, but this is not the case. Consistently over the past five years only 13 of the 20 Premiership clubs have employed chartered physiotherapists.

Of the clubs in the Premiership in 1995 the following trusted their primary medical care to the FA and its diploma: Aston Villa, Everton, Nottingham Forest, Coventry, Wimbledon, Queens Park Rangers and Manchester City. Clubs have come and gone from the top flight since, but at the start of the 1998-99 season there were still seven Premiership clubs without a full-time chartered physiotherapist on their books.

In all only 38 of the 92 clubs employ chartered physio-therapists. Indeed there are probably more chartered physio-therapists working in non-league football than there are in professional football. Non-league clubs, because they cannot afford full-time medical staff, have arrangements with chartered practices during the season. So, many of the bodies of the most expensive athletes in the land upon whom depend the hopes and dreams of millions, never mind the fortunes of clubs, rely for their primary health care on people who, in the main, are minimally qualified to do the job.

So why do so many clubs put their faith in the FA and its

diploma when it is clearly in the interest of a football club to have the best available medical care on hand for its players? Essentially it springs from a widespread distrust of any expert who does not come with a footballing pedigree. For all the media attention and scrutiny, the football world remains a closed one. To import people perceived to be non-footballing folk and put them in a position where they can challenge the team management, with opinions based on considered expertise, is something many clubs are simply not used to and find difficult to accept.

The prevailing view in football clubs still using FA diploma-qualified physiotherapists is that what their man lacks in general medical knowledge, he makes up for with intimate knowledge of footballers and the football club. As with the famous Liverpool 'boot-room', traditionally the physiotherapist has been seen as part of the fabric of the club. More often than not grateful for the job, the physiotherapists role has extended far beyond mere medical matters.

Martin Haines remembers his first experience in a football club: 'I knew a club physiotherapist and asked if I could come down and have a look at what his job involved. Basically, apart from treating players, he was also laying out the kit, booking the hotel and, as often as not, loading all the luggage on to the coach which he had probably hired. That was a long time ago, but I would be surprised if it had changed much in the lower divisions.'

Roger Wylde sympathizes with the view that an understanding of football culture is crucial to any physiotherapist aspiring to work in football. In a career spanning 15 years Roger played for a dozen football clubs both home and abroad. The high point of his career in this country would probably be his spell at Sheffield Wednesday. After he finished playing he took the FA diploma, but then went on to become a fully-chartered physiotherapist: 'I just felt I wanted to know more. It was hard work but ultimately very satisfying because being chartered means something'.

He qualified on a course aimed at ex-footballers at Salford University and now works for Stockport County. Despite having taken the trouble to become fully qualified himself, even Roger Wylde subscribes to the view that a footballing man is preferable to a physiotherapist fresh from the NHS.

'You cannot have chartered physiotherapists from a hospital background beating the drum and getting on their high horse saying that you have to be chartered. You *have* got to be that. But do they know what a footballer's requirements are? They can't come out of hospital and say: "Yes, I know what a footballer requires", because they have *no* idea what a footballer requires.'

Certainly there are some important differences between what is required of a hospital physiotherapist and a football one. For a start there is no need to force-march a pensioner who has undergone a hip replacement operation back to tip-top condition; the rehabilitation process would be carried out at the patient's pace. But the whole point of physiotherapy in football is to return the player as good as new as quickly as possible.

But does Roger Wylde's contention stand up to scrutiny? If someone aspires to work in football it may be reasonable to assume that it is a work culture they would feel comfortable with and could thrive in. The fact that someone like Roger Wylde, with experience on both sides of the fence, should still feel the need to defend the football tribe is an indication of how deep- rooted the difficulty is of creating a modern healthcare system for footballers. And Roger feels this way even though he has had personal experiences of a club's care which sent him scurrying to the nearest private physiotherapist when he needed treatment.

'I can remember as a player – but I am not prepared to say where – joining a club where the groundsman took over as physiotherapist, which I thought was pretty amazing.'

Further investigation revealed that the club in question was Barnsley, late of the Premier League, and that the groundsman had retired by the time the team made it to the top flight. He had successfully completed the FA Diploma and I have no evidence to suggest anything other than that he carried out his duties with due diligence and competence. Neeedless to say, though, the sight of a man marking lines one moment and manipulating muscles the next, raised some eyebrows among the senior players.

One of the reasons why chartered physiotherapists are, if not frowned upon, certainly sometimes regarded with suspicion, is the trouble they can cause for a manager. Only now as football clubs begin to employ professional management teams to run their business is the power of the manager beginning to wane.

In the heyday of the likes of Bill Shankly, Brian Clough and Matt Busby, nothing much happened at their clubs without their say and this often extended to deciding if a player was fit to play or not. The advantage of employing a physiotherapist who had difficulty divining the difference between a strain and a break is that he is hardly likely to blind you with science. A chartered physiotherapist, however, would doubtless argue the case from well-founded knowledge.

'You have to be a strong character,' says Martin Haines. 'The manager and the management team want the players back on the park yesterday, but this is not always the best thing for the player, or indeed the long-term interests of the club. You were often caught between the manager and the best interests of the player.'

Stuart Robson says that in his experience it was not unusual for the manager to decide who was and who was not fit and then instruct the physiotherapist accordingly: 'The manager sometimes says we want this player fit by Saturday or we do not want this player fit because we do not want to pick him, so tell him he has got to have another week on the treatment table.'

Stuart Robson's charge that players are regarded as club property finds resonance with Liverpool's Tommy Smith when he thinks back on a rather less-well-known piece of Shankly wisdom. It was an utterance which came when the defender suggested he might wear a bandage on his thigh during a game. Again it was a conversation conducted through the medium of the physiotherapist at the time, Joe Fagan.

Smith to Shankly: 'My thigh is still a bit sore, but I think I could play if I wore a bandage.'

Shankly to Fagan: 'Tell him, Joe. He has got no chance of playing.'

Fagan to Smith: 'The boss says you have no chance of playing if you wear a bandage.'

Smith to Fagan: 'Tell him to sod off. It is not his leg, it's mine.'

Shankly to Smith: (breaking his golden rule of never speaking to an injured player) 'Oh, no, son. You are wrong, son. It is not your leg. It is Liverpool Football Club's leg.'

It was an ankle belonging to Bournemouth Football Club that put paid to a promising career of the elder son of a famous footballing family. Mark Redknapp, Harry's son and Jamie's brother. Mark was a defender with the south-coast outfit just about the time Jamie was making his début. In a reserve clash with Cardiff, he went into a tackle and came out of it with an injury that left him on crutches.

The diagnosis was that it was ligament damage and Mark was treated accordingly. Over a period of 18 months he attempted come-back after come-back, first with Bournemouth and then later with a number of non-league sides. Each time he broke down. After two years of heartache he eventually went to see a specialist who discovered the root cause of the problem.

'I was playing with a broken ankle for over a year and my club physiotherapist didn't realize it was broken. It was only after I had X-ray after X-ray that I realized it was a shattered bone. It does make me bitter when I think about it, but I now have a decent job that's going quite well and it keeps me away from thinking about football.'

Mark is now a football agent, representing the interests of Rio Ferdinand among others. He has something of his father's wheeler- dealer ability and thoroughly enjoys his job, but it does not stop him thinking, what if?

'I would have loved to be a footballer. I go and watch them at the training ground and I feel very envious. I look at them and think that is what I wanted to be, but then I switch off and say it is not going to happen. I may have made it at lower level. I may have made it at Premier League, but it is not to be so I just get on with life now.'

The list of players who have fallen foul of by the ludicrous fumblings of poorly-qualified physiotherapists would probably fill several volumes. But there is a difficulty in documenting them. Players whose careers are finished by injury usually collect an insurance pay-out. There is little financial incentive to go to the law and pursue a damages claim if it is thought that misdiagnosis was the cause of a player having to quit the game. In assessing the quality of physiotherapy in football we are left with anecdotes and the fact that increasingly, players do seek private care rather than trust themselves to their clubs. Players like Andy (not his real name). He has been a journeyman player with several clubs that have bounced around the lower leagues in the past decade. He's still playing, but for the last five years whenever he has been injured he has gone private.

'The major problem with these people (non-chartered physiotherapists) is that they only ever treat footballers – and many of the injuries are probably quite familiar. Then – because they are not properly qualified – if anything slightly unusual comes their way they do not have the experience, like a hospital physiotherapist does, of treating different kinds of injuries, and quite frankly they are lost. They just hope for the best.'

By chance, Andy made a friend of a chartered physiotherapist in Luton, and she quickly realized that, like Mark Redknapp, the ankle strain Andy was being treated for was in fact a break. From that day on, Andy has never trusted a club physiotherapist unless he or she is chartered.

'The clubs that I have been involved with, have two, three, maybe four pieces of equipment. Whatever injury you have, you seem to get the same treatment. They will put you on one machine, followed by another and then a third. If it is a different injury they might vary the order. They just seem to think that by having machines they have to use them.'

Such a scenario makes John Green at West Ham splutter with anger. 'The science relating to physiotherapy is changing all the time. Many of the techniques I was taught on my course have now been re-thought and some are out of date. I am across these changes because I make sure I keep up to date with developments through my professional association. Take ultra-sound machines, the way we use them now is completely different to say five years ago. The idea of someone applying ultra-sound with no proper training makes my blood boil.'

Like Stuart Robson, Andy says that since his eyes were opened by his friend the chartered physiotherapist, he has directed dozens of players to go private.

Eamonn Salmon, a chartered physiotherapist in Nelson, East Lancashire, is one of the many physiotherapists seeing footballers on the quiet. Having once worked for a Premier League club, Eamonn knows all about the stresses and strains footballers experience. He was hired by Peter Reid to look after Manchester City in the early 1990s, replacing the club's non-chartered physiotherapist, Roy Bailey.

'At the time I joined,' he said, 'I was surprised by the equipment in the treatment room. I thought it must be the latest gear because I had never seen much of it before. It was only later when I checked with my books that I realized the reason I had never seen it before was that is was so out of date. It was functional, but I did feel that if I was going to do my job correctly at a Premier League club then I needed the best equipment.'

Peter Reid was happy to oblige and the Manchester City treatment room was duly kitted out. By the time Peter Reid was sacked and Alan Ball came in, Salmon had tired of the football business and left to set up his own practice

'It was an eye-opener to be honest. I had no preconceived ideas but I quite quickly realized there were people who were not qualified working within the game. And I was surprised to find that there was no maxim from the FA that all clubs should have a chartered physiotherapist.'

Salmon's experience highlights another problem football has with physiotherapy – holding on to a chartered physiotherapist. The going rate for a physiotherapist in the Premiership is around £40,000, and with win-bonuses this can rise to around £70,000. For the majority outside the Premiership, however, £30,000 a year would be pushing it. A chartered physiotherapist in private practice could earn more than this and work more sensible hours to boot. The very top clubs, for obvious reasons, have less of a problem.

If you work at a football club, it effectively means no holidays for ten months of the year, long hours travelling around the country to away fixtures, and even in the summer break the chances are you will be called in to deal with long-term treatment cases, never mind supervising the pre-season training.

David Swift, the Leeds physiotherapist, managed a hospital physiotherapy unit before arriving at the Premier League Club. He agrees he works long hours: 'I am lucky at Leeds because we have a team of three physiotherapists, but even so I only ever have one day off a week and that is rarely at weekends because we are usually playing. To have two days off in a row is a rare luxury.'

For people like Eamonn Salmon, this was no life, so he quit. (Incidentally, Alan Ball then re-hired the non-chartered Roy Bailey, who is still at Maine Road.)

Although the likes of John Green at West Ham see no alternative to employing chartered physiotherapists at clubs, for others – like Martin Haines and Roger Wylde at Stockport – there is room for compromise. Martin Haines believes that the FA Diploma man has a place pitch-side, if he's working as a chartered physiotherapist's assistant and preferably has every intention of wanting to go on to be chartered.

'Certainly from the first-aid point of view these guys are very good, but when it comes to the specifics of diagnosis and progressing through to full rehabilitation that is when your qualified physiotherapist can and should come in.'

If the Football Association has difficulty imposing change on the clubs, the Professional Footballers Association (PFA) is a different matter. With 100 per cent membership at professional clubs and as the biggest footballers' agent organization in the country, it has the power to bring pressure to bear on clubs through its members.

Certainly according to leading football agent, John Holmes, it is in a position to push the case for chartered physiotherapy care for its members: 'It would be a worthy object of the PFA's attention. It is one of the richest institutions in soccer. And it seems to me that it has a very good chance to put pressure on.'

The PFA certainly has a clear policy of wanting clubs to

employ chartered physiotherapists and has backed this up by co-funding two university courses, aimed at former footballers attaining chartered qualifications. It is hoped that, by the end of the year 2000, 36 students will swell the ranks of chartered physiotherapists in football thanks to courses run at Salford University and Kings College, London.

Professional sport in this country has long had a diffident attitude to sports medicine in general, of which the problem with physiotherapy in football is just the most obvious manifestation. The whole medical structure surrounding football clubs has for years been a messy affair. Doctors and surgeons with an interest in sport simply offered themselves to football clubs in much the same way as local businessmen inveigled their way on to the board or perhaps became chairman.

For some a connection with a football club was not just a mere glamorous honorarium but good for business, too. If you are treating a superstar's knee, groin or ankle, that would be recommendation enough for your run-of-the mill private patient with money to spend on elective surgery to correct similar ailments.

This state of affairs has arisen because of the nature of our National Health Service. One consequence of a health service funded by the taxpayer is there are cash limits on treatments that can be offered. Traditionally, sports injuries have been considered self-inflicted by the medical profession and placed in much the same class as cosmetic surgery. Crucially there is also no Royal College of Sport Physicians.

The purpose of a medical Royal College is to ensure taxpayers get value for money by setting standards in training and research. Effectively, this means that only disciplines supported by a Royal College are available on the NHS (or in the case of non-medical disciplines like physiotherapy, an equivalent standards organization). UK medical students cannot qualify as sports medicine specialists. They can only choose to develop an enthusiasm for treating people with sports injuries once they are qualified in another discipline.

There are medics from all disciplines who are interested

in sports medicine and they have their own association, BASM (British Association of Sports Medicine), but its status is little more than that of a club. Then there is the additional problem of some members of the Royal Colleges – most obviously orthopaedics (bones) or physiologists – who actively oppose the development of sports medicine as a separate discipline because they consider it an impingement.

In Europe and the United States, specialists develop according to the demand in the market place. The treatment of sport injuries is big business and consequently European medical schools are full of medical students aspiring to be sports medicine specialists.

The whole medical infrastructure at Continental sports clubs reflects the medical culture at large, and the likes of Barcelona or Bayern Munich have a large medical team, including doctors, surgeons and physiotherapists on the pay roll.

In the United States such is the commercial value of a contract with a sports team that medical practices actually pay the club to treat its stars, the pay-off being the prestige, publicity and astronomical fees they can subsequently charge members of the general public who flock to them with sport-related injuries.

Given the value of players, clubs should not be content merely with chartered physiotherapists but the best chartered physiotherapists. As it is, too many professional footballers are in the hands of people who could – and should – be better qualified. Adam Brown, formerly of the Football Supporters' Association, believes physiotherapy at football clubs is now a consumer issue.

'The key issue here is that fans are being asked to pay more and more to watch football yet clubs do not seem to be investing that money into the long-term interests of their product or players.'

Certainly if a squad, ravaged by injury, is in addition handicapped by poor diagnosis and rehabilitation, then fans have every right to be angry when their teams lose out on trophies, or are relegated as a result of skimping on the physiotherapy budget.

One aspect of the increase – and influence – of foreign players in the English leagues is that our home-grown stars are waking up to the kind of care they should be receiving, and are making their own arrangements, even if these involve subterfuge. One leading sports physiotherapist, lately retired from caring for the squad of one of our national teams, says that half of his business now comes from professional footballers disillusioned with their club's physiotherapist.

The pressure to do something about the pitiful state of medical care in professional football probably means that the days of the FA diploma man are numbered but not, one suspects, before a few final anomalies.

One such anomaly – the brain child of Howard Wilkinson, the FA's Technical Director – has been thrown up by the FA's plan for junior football academies at professional clubs. Wilkinson – who has long been a believer in chartered physiotherapists at football clubs and who employed them exclusively when he was a manager – has made it an FA sanction condition to operate junior academies at professional football clubs, and that the club must employ a chartered physiotherapist to look after the youngsters.

Excellent idea though this is, it would seem that there is now a chance that some junior club youngsters will be looked after by someone who is better qualified than the physiotherapist in charge of the first team.

As they like to say in football, 'It's a funny old game'.

It should be noted that Liverpool Football Club now employ chartered physiotherapists.

CHAPTER FIVE

Hunting the Hooligans
With the Undercover Police at France 98

Ten days before the start of the 1998 World Cup finals, a group of men in expensive but casual designer clothes meet at a secret location in the English Midlands. They are veterans of violent disorder at scores of football grounds and are plotting a trip to France. They decide the logistics of their travel and accommodation, choosing hotels outside city centres to avoid detection, discussing which hooligan leaders they are likely to meet, speculating which games are most likely to spark aggro. They have little chance of enjoying the hospitality and unique atmosphere of a great sporting event. They are not going for the football; they're going for the trouble.

The men are Football Intelligence Officers (FIOs), known colloquially as 'spotters', and their meeting place is a high-security police station in Nottingham. They have been chosen – in a selection process every bit as tense as Glen Hoddle's choice for his England squad – to form an élite team to travel to France. There, they will help the *gendarmerie* meet the threat posed by the world's worst soccer thugs.

Most are detective constables hand-picked from the ranks of England's county and metropolitan forces. Week in, week out, they gather information about hooligan gangs which they then use to prevent fights and build evidence. Often their work goes unseen.

'Sometimes we go back to the police commander at the end of the day and he'll say, "Well, nothing happened, that was a nice quiet day". And then we explain that something *was* planned but it was all averted by our policing operation,' says one of them.

'We first sent Football Intelligence Officers abroad as spotters in 1990 for the World Cup,' says assistant Chief Constable Tim Hollis, the man responsible for the policing of football in England and Wales. 'Since then we've built up a team of international spotters, local FIOs with their own forces, who have developed a level of expertise and knowledge of fans who cause disorder on a wider scale.'

At Nottingham, the all-male team was briefed by Detective Chief Superintendent Eddie Curtis, who would lead them in France. He was chosen partly because of his wide policing experience – including the violent disorder of the Miners' Strike in the early 1980s – and partly because he speaks fluent French. Given the proximity of the tournament – a short trip through the Channel Tunnel – and the presence of other clubs with active hooligans such as Germany, Holland, Belgium, Italy and Argentina, he knew he was likely to be under considerable pressure, but his manner was relaxed and jokey.

There would be a lot riding on the spotters and some were feeling the strain. One detective constable with a key intelligence-collating role confided that he couldn't sleep for a week before the tournament because of 'worry and stress'.

For all of them, though, the trip was a career peak. The oldest member of the team was Jack, a weathered, pipe-smoking northerner who turned down a professional rugby league offer to join the police. Now, just months away from retirement, France 98 was to be the icing on the cake. 'It has to be the top, hasn't it? Most FIOs would give their right arms to be in the position that we are. I've been looking forward to it from the day I got the telephone call to say I was going.'

Jack normally policed a lower-division club with a relatively small following. His typical Saturday duty would be crowd control at some wind-blown Third Division outpost. He was selected for France because of the notoriety of their active hooligan element.

'Although we are a small club, they are big contenders on the England scene for the international hooligan. They're well-known throughout the hooligan world. They go abroad a lot, and quite a few of them have been arrested abroad and deported.'

Although they wear plain clothes abroad, at home the spotters work in uniform, filming crowds or speaking to fans at games. They gather titbits from informants and other sources and phone each other before games to swap knowledge and draw up a match-day plan. Bill, from a Midlands force, has been trailing the thugs for 15 years and once spent months undercover infiltrating a particularly violent gang.

'It's a cat-and-mouse game. We're the cats – and I've never yet seen a mouse eat a cat. You follow the intelligence as it is occurring – normally by the minute – and just follow your nose, follow your instinct. It's like a hunt.'

Such is the secrecy of their work that, until permission was given for *On The Line* to follow the team in France, no media organization had ever been allowed to accompany the international spotters on duty.

What follows is a unique insider's account of what happened there. Restrictions on revealing the names and number of the spotters have been respected. Otherwise this is the unvarnished diary of France 98: the Spotters' Story.

Saturday, 13 June
Most of the spotting team fly to Marseilles, the host city for England's first game against Tunisia. No sooner have they landed than they are out on the streets, helping the French police to deal with a disturbance in the Old Port area, where several hundred England fans are drinking. Trouble flares again at the end of the night when a British fan falls off a car and is hit by another vehicle. Policing is complicated by factors beyond the spotters' control: the second biggest city in France has a high crime rate, a tough reputation and simmering racial tensions among its large North African immigrant community.

Sunday, 14 June
The FA's security adviser, Sir Brian Hayes, plays down the previous night's bother at a well-attended morning press

conference. 'I think it's important to keep everything in proportion. It's a big busy town, there was drinking and rowdy behaviour, a few bottles thrown. At the end of the day there were four people arrested. Two have been released. In the general run of things it was a minor incident.'

Down on the narrow Prado beach that afternoon, rival fans mingled peacefully in the sunshine beside a giant TV screen. There was little hint of what was to follow – what one spotter called 'the worst violence I have ever witnessed'.

By early evening a boozy English hard core was massing at a waterfront bar called O'Malleys. Some then left the pub and tried to burn an Irish flag before chanting, 'No Surrender to the IRA'. That soon turned to, 'Come on, let's do the Old Bill'.

A spotter takes up the story. 'We and a French police officer decided to try and identify certain people up there. We were in amongst them when they recognized that we were police officers and suddenly wanted to attack us. Perhaps not having the guts to do it physically they started chucking bottles and all sorts of things at us. We were chased, stoned and bottled and had to make a tactical retreat... but if we hadn't done that some of us might not be here to tell the tale.'

A volley of tear-gas stopped the pursuing louts in their tracks. Noxious clouds drifted through Marseilles' restaurant quarter, leaving innocent diners spluttering into their shellfish. It was to be the first of many barrages that evening.

Dressed in civvies, the spotters had no visible means of identifying themselves and, despite their French 'minders', were sometimes mistaken for hooligans by the heavily-armed riot police. 'At one stage the French police thought they were English hooligans, the local youths thought they were English hooligans, and English hooligans knew they were spotters,' said Eddie Curtis, 'so they came under attack from all three sides.'

A forty-yard no man's land opened up between the riot squad in helmets, shields and body armour and the English fans in shorts and polo shirts. Some of the hooligans picked up chairs, bottles and sticks and hurled them at the police lines. One of the dozens of press cameramen swarming around like mosquitoes ventured too close; he was punched, kicked and chased off.

The attitude of the French police, who simply stood their ground, firing tear-gas when the hooligans got too close, bemused their English colleagues. There was little attempt to disperse the fans or to make arrests. Still, it gave the English team plenty of opportunities to video the ensuing riot with their hand-held cameras.

Finally, after two hours of tear-gas and taunts that would be shown on news broadcasts around the world, the police made their move, marching forward in a line and banging their shields like Zulus. The hooligans tried to gee each other up to stand their ground but when the police broke into a charge the fans fled, leaving broken windows and an overturned car in their wake.

Meanwhile, on the other side of the harbour, scores of Arab youths and some of Marseilles' own soccer hooligans engaged in a pitched battle with a small group of English. The ground was soon littered with broken glass. Anyone caught alone was brutally beaten. One man was trapped down a side street and his throat was cut. Several of the spotters and a plain-clothes French colleague were caught up in the terror.

'We were with a father and son from Leeds who were terrified and we were trying to get them to safety. There was panic when tear-gas was fired at the crowd and we ran into an alley to get away. We were confronted by thirty to forty French youths. They thought we were English football supporters. It was very dangerous. I thought we were going to get stabbed.

'Then the French police officer pulled out his ID. They backed off but you could tell they were frustrated. They said to us, "You tell the English hooligans, the fucking French hooligans are still alive. We are waiting for you". This group then attacked English supporters who were outside a hotel. After this, they moved on to a bar where there were English and attacked that group as well, causing a number of injuries.'

The bar owner and a powerfully-built but terrified bouncer pulled down a metal shutter to keep out local thugs who were trying to smash their way in to attack the English. By midnight, the darkness was split by the blue flashing lights of police vehicles. The acrid tang of tear-gas was everywhere, glass and debris littered the streets. And some of the gangs were still fighting.

'We came upon a number of English supporters who had been stabbed and slashed with knives,' says a London officer. 'A number were saying they were just trying to get back to their hotels. They were almost fighting for their lives. We attempted to move them away but, in our view, it was clear that everywhere they went they were being attacked.'

Monday, 15 June
As Eddie Curtis and his men watched their video evidence the next day, they realized they had spectacular material which would be used repeatedly over the following weeks to arrest and convict the ringleaders. 'After filming this sort of stuff for the past 15 years, that was probably the best evidence I've ever filmed,' said one of the team.

Police forces worldwide grade soccer thugs in to three categories: A, B and C. The worst are Category C, those who organize violence, and Category B, those most likely to join in. There are judged to be about 200 Category Cs on the England international scene.

For the match, Detective Chief Superintendent Curtis split his team into small groups, each tasked with watching a different area of the city, and briefed them on the day's tactics: 'If there's anybody selling tickets on the black market, tell your French colleagues. They're going to lock them up and take their tickets. If we've got any Category Cs and Category Bs on the beach, ask them if they've got tickets.'

Each group then piled into an unmarked Renault Espace people-carrier, driven by the French officers who were their constant companions, and headed off, meeting later at the Stade Velodrome. Their first stop was at a garage, to stock up on chocolate bars: such had been the frenzy of their first 48 hours on foreign soil that few of the spotters had been able to grab a proper meal; one group claimed to have eaten only a large bag of Bombay Mix brought over from the UK.

Inside the Stade Velodrome, their job was to watch the crowd, film some faces with hand held cameras and try to pick out any people from the disorder the previous night. A valuable source of information were the flags, revealing the names of home towns and clubs, that many England followers display.

There was some sporadic skirmishing outside the ground, but most of the trouble that day occurred by the big screen on the beach after England scored the first of the two goals that would secure them victory. Several innocent people were injured by missiles. The atmosphere that evening was tense, but there were few further clashes as most of the England contingent either left the city or stayed away from the Old Port area. Still, the spotters were out until well after midnight.

Tuesday, 16 June
The spotters' first downtime. After helping to take statements from some of those being held at Marseilles police station, the officers are invited to another station at a small beach near the resort. Lunch was followed by beach volleyball and a spot of sunbathing, the pale white bodies of the English force a comic contrast to the well-tanned locals. Even then, a couple of the group spent the afternoon hunched over a laptop, feeding in information on some of their target 'faces' seen over the weekend.

Although unanimous in their condemnation of the trouble, the spotters were well aware that the majority of England fans in Marseilles had not been involved. 'It's important to put things in perspective,' said one. 'We must have been looking, at a conservative estimate, at 10-15,000 England fans in the stadium. Even at the height of the Sunday night trouble there were only 300 involved, and only a few of these were deliberately provoking disorder, maybe as few as 150. So we are talking about a significantly low figure.'

Not everyone blamed the English. At least one French bar gave free drinks to Brits for fighting with the local Arabs, a reflection of racial antagonism in an area where the right-wing *Front National* is popular. Paris police sergeant Jean Paul Tarot, who was with the English spotters, was objective. 'The world's

Press say it's the English, always the English, but in France you have the problem with the French Arabs. The problem was fifty-fifty, not just the English people.'

Some of the spotters head off to Montpelier, where Italy are playing, to check out information that English gangs might be there.

Wednesday-Friday, 17-19 June
Much of the spotters' time was spent on the road, swilling warm bottles of mineral water and listening to tapes of football songs; long periods of *ennui* that contrasted vividly with the adrenaline-pumping excitement of crowd control. The drive from Marseilles to Toulouse took them from a noisy Mediterranean melting pot to a cosmopolitan city of smart cafés and art shops. They were greeted by good-natured groups of fans drinking in the main square, the *Place du Capitole*, and by the news that special powers had been introduced by the French authorities to allow the immediate expulsion of any Category C thugs.

'The police can detain suspects for four hours, and if we look at their record and see they have a long record of violence, particularly at football matches, we will point that out and the local French prefect will decide if that person can stay,' said Eddie Curtis. 'If he considers that person a danger then he will send him home.'

These new legal powers were just what the spotters had wanted.

Saturday, 20 June
The spotters toured Toulouse with their French colleagues and set up a couple of secret observation points. Little sign of trouble.

Sunday, 21 June
To relieve them of some of the organizational burden, the team was joined by a French-speaking logistics officer from the Metropolitan Police, DCI Kevin Hurley. He briefed them on the new powers at the main police station – where a large armour-plated water-cannon was parked ominously in the forecourt.

'Okay, you are going to be followed around by a plain-clothes arrest team. The idea is for you to identify anyone who is a Category C. We are going to bring them in like before, but then they will go through immediate emergency expulsion. Just say they are Category C, *arrêtez-lui*, and they will. You can all say that, can't you?'

It was to be a day not of arrests however, but of fight-prevention. The first incident happened that afternoon in the café-lined main square, where hundreds of good-natured England fans were milling around. Three local Arab youths took it upon themselves to hurl insults at one group of supporters and, as the English lads walked over to confront them, one of the youths brandished a large stick.

Three of the spotters were filming the incident, but when they realized it could blow up into violence, they quickly called in the French police. Within seconds the local youth was arrested and – probably for the first and only time in their careers – the spotters were treated to a round of applause from the England fans.

The outcome was in stark contrast to events perpetrated the same day by German thugs in the northern French town of Lens; a helmeted and armed gendarme was beaten into a coma with a paving stone. Rumours – which later proved false – circulated that he had died. So when 300 England fans became a nuisance outside a bar called the Melting Pot, dozens of grim-faced CRS riot police in the now-familiar Robocop gear lined up a few hundred yards down the road and prepared to charge.

The spotters were also rushed to the scene. 'There was a problem when the English spilled on to the road,' said one. 'There must have been 100 or more in the road, all of them had been drinking and they were obviously blocking the road. I was wearing the same as the other lads: shorts and T-shirt, but by now we'd been given armbands so the French police would know who we were.'

In a bid to prevent mayhem, the French commander asked DCI Hurley if his men would mediate with the fans and get them to move. Not all of the spotters were happy: they had no protective clothing and no powers of arrest in a foreign country. Still, they fanned out across the dark street and tried to persuade the fans to move. 'Come on lads, keep out of the road now. Let the traffic through!'

While some of the revellers began to move away, others were very drunk and trying to incite the rest to attack the police. A few bottles and glasses were thrown. Not for the first time, the situation was made worse by the presence of photographers and reporters who used the advancing British officers as cover to approach the crowd and take pictures. They, rather than the police, became an immediate target for attack, with the spotters caught in the middle.

Eventually, as the French police marched up in ranks with batons drawn, the spotters were forced to back away. The road was cleared without unnecessary force and, in the event, only one man was arrested, then quickly released after a sobbing protest from his girlfriend. It was another successful and relatively peaceful operation, but not all the officers were happy.

'To be fair, some of the lads thought we were put in an unnecessary situation. With hindsight the operation worked well and we did help the French police, but I don't think any of us would want to be put in that situation again. We definitely felt vulnerable.'

Which was a diplomatic way of saying that some of the spotters were angry at being exposed. There was some plain-speaking that night behind closed doors. Commanding officer Eddie Curtis acknowledged his men's vulnerability, but supported the decision to send them in.

'They certainly did feel exposed. But the person responsible on the ground took a calculated decision that there were not any really nasty people in that crowd who would have been able to whip up violence.'

Monday, 22 June
England v Romania. Kick-off is not until early evening but one of the English police team is at the stadium from noon. Phil works for the National Criminal Intelligence Service (NCIS),

which collates intelligence on serious criminals ranging from gangsters to sex offenders. Football hooligan gangs also fall within its remit.

In a meeting room under one of the stands he sets up a TV set and laptop computer. He has two mobile phones, one to connect his computer to the Internet and the other to field calls from his colleagues out on the streets. As they phone in with sightings of particular faces, he keys the information into a running log and also e-mails the NCIS HQ in London, where they check criminal records and files on Category C targets on a computer system called 'Goalkeeper'.

The laptop and modem are on loan from computer firm Hewlett Packard; neither the Home Office, the FA nor the British police were prepared pay for the electronic hardware that was necessary to support an international intelligence operation. (The spotters even had to buy their own team polo shirts.)

'The lads can ring in to me, I'm in electronic contact with my office back in England and can make various requests. The replies are then sent back to me,' says Phil. 'We have a nice little database including photos of most of our major subjects. I can type in a club and can immediately highlight the Category Cs.'

Phil is to spend ten hours in his underground nerve-centre, keeping the lines of intelligence flowing. He leaves his desk only once – to join the crowd for a rousing version of 'God Save The Queen' just before the kick off. 'It made the hairs stand up on the back of my neck,' he says later.

Despite defeat for England, the atmosphere at the ground is incredibly upbeat and there is no trouble. Later the spotters visit the main train station; scores of Brits are crashed out on the concourse, sleeping off their hangovers. Phil arrives back at his hotel well after midnight. The bar is full of celebrating Romanians who have drunk all the beer.

Tuesday, 23 June
The morning is spent souvenir shopping and sight-seeing in Toulouse. Then it's off on the long drive north to Lens for England's crucial game against Colombia. The tired team now

face the longest journey of the trip: two hot days on the road in people- carriers, after a string of long days and late nights in low-rent accommodation (one of the hotels they had been booked into was so bad that the spotters took one look and walked straight out again). It is the natural time for morale to flag. Things are not helped when one of the French police drivers, a woman constable from Paris, decides to go into a massive and inexplicable Gallic huff, a mood that will last until the end of the tournament.

Wednesday, 24 June
Lens is hardly likely to lift spirits. A series of conical slag heaps greets visitors to this dull, provincial mining town which even the bunting and flags cannot brighten. Some of the spotters meet up for an evening beer with Dutch police mates they have worked with on previous trips. They swap stories and black humour.

Thursday, 25 June
Twenty miles from Lens is the bigger and busier city of Lille. With its Channel Tunnel terminal, it is going to be the embarkation point for most of the England fans. Thousands are expected, many without tickets, as this game is the easiest to reach of England's first-round matches. The spotters also have intelligence from colleagues watching at ports and train stations that this fixture is likely to attract the heaviest hooligan groups.

In one Lille bar packed with drinking Brits, the spotters identify two Category C targets. They phone in to check their criminal records; under the new powers, the men can be kicked out of the country if their convictions are serious enough. The problem is that any attempt to enter the bar and grab them could spark a riot.

'The French police wanted to go straight in, but we told them to wait until the men left. Eventually, after two hours, they came out in a group of six. We had checked their previous convictions and established that one of the two could be kicked out of the country. Unfortunately, because they're identical twins, we had to take both back to the police station to ascertain which one was which.'

Their softly-softly approach is well-placed. For, over the next twenty-four hours, Lille is to see a gathering of some of the most formidable hooligans gangs, many of them veterans of hundreds of street brawls.

'These, for want of a better phrase, are the better quality of hooligan,' says one spotter. 'Those in Marseilles and Toulouse were more the English-lads-in-Benidorm type, lads away for their holidays together. Here, there hasn't been the singing in the streets, there are not as many England shirts, not as many flags, and the people seem to be watching the streets rather than watching each other. They're more streetwise. At the first sign of disorder they disperse and re-group later somewhere else. They don't stand there to be picked-off by the police or identified by the TV cameras. It's a hit-and-run mentality.'

All the more worrying, then, to find that the police chief at Lille is not expecting the British spotting team, and had only 45 officers on duty the night before the match – the number you would expect for an average Saturday night in Hull or Brighton. This leads to a lively debate with DCI Kevin Hurley.

'I've discovered there are no CRS [riot police] or Brigade Gendarmerie Mobil deployed here. They are effectively the public-order police, the men with shields and helmets. I have expressed the view that they might like some on reserve. The French have discussed it and are calling up a company of CRS officers, just under ninety people, to be on standby. I don't think they are aware of the potential difficulties here. They suspect the problems may be in Lens tomorrow.'

The Lille officers, however, do not let their lack of numbers dampen their enthusiasm. By mid-evening the Police Commissariat is filling up with English prisoners, many of them drunk. Each is filmed by the spotters, who also help the French take down their details. Most of the fans are drunk, stroppy and uncooperative.

One particularly offensive trouble-maker takes exception to the possibility that 'They're gonna put us on some fuckin' register'. Despite being handcuffed he lunges across the police car at the spotter who is filming him and has to be restrained by French police. Yet the spotters have found from experience that English hooligans arrested in a foreign country often undergo a remarkable transformation in their attitude to the British police.

'When you're abroad, and they find themselves in police custody and think they may be facing jail, they suddenly become your best friend. They say to you, "Oh, English old Bill, thank God you're here". The same person back home would want to smack you in the mouth. We had one who was arrested for being drunk and wanting to fight the world, but in the back of the car he kept saying, "I can't take this. My wife will leave me. I'll lose my job," and he was in tears, like a big baby.'

By the end of the night there have been around 50 arrests but no serious trouble.

Friday, 26 June
The spotters split up, some going to Lens, some snooping around Lille train station, others setting up a secret observation post in Lille city centre. From a first-floor office, the men – equipped with binoculars and a video camera – have a bird's-eye view of the soccer gangs which, in the absence of any local opposition, begin to weigh each other up.

'In one small bar we've got confirmed sitings of Wolverhampton and Huddersfield hooligans, a German who has been seen quite a few times with the English, and possibly some Chelsea hooligans,' says Bill. 'There are too many to take anybody out at this time. That would just cause really serious disorder.'

Suddenly a short, sharp fight breaks out between a member of the so-called Newcastle Gremlins gang and a muscular bruiser with no shirt on. It is over almost as soon as it starts, with the out-punched Newcastle fan and his mates moving reluctantly away.

'One small incident like that could start an awful lot of trouble. If the police went in, it would just escalate and probably everyone in the square would get involved in a mass riot.'

There are other minor incidents as some of the rowdier

English fans seek to confront the police. Eventually the fans suss out the observation post. They wave and make crude gestures. The spotters decide it is time to go.

Thousands without tickets watch the game that evening on French TV in bars. England win and go through. A ban on booze in Lens contributes to a largely trouble-free night. But one young England follower misses the post-match celebrations when his past crimes catch up with him.

'He was first caught on film throwing bottles towards the police lines in the port area of Marseilles. He didn't just throw one, he threw a box. He was videoed and we made a paste-up on the computer and put him down as "Wanted". We then saw him in Toulouse after we were called to another disturbance, but he noticed us first and ran. On the way he was changing his clothing. We were hoping that we were going to get him in Lens and, sure enough, we went to a small skirmish outside Lens stadium and saw him coming up the road towards us. We informed our French colleagues and they detained him.'

Saturday, 27 June
The spotters show the French police the video evidence they have on the arrested man. Anthony Winstone, from Fulham, is later jailed for four months, the last of the Marseilles riot ringleaders to be caught. It highlights the usefulness of small hand-held cameras – the greatest tools in the spotters' armoury. As Jack explains:

'The hooligans don't like the video camera. They'll do anything to get away from it. They'll cover their heads, wear dark glasses, wear hats, bonnets, collars up, anything. Because once they're on film, if anything goes wrong, they know they can be identified.'

Bill and a colleague once prevented two gangs fighting by standing between them and filming. 'It was like Custer's Last Stand. Two large groups of hooligans were about to attack each other. They started running forward and we found ourselves filming in the middle, working back to back. As the groups ran towards each other they saw us and stopped, almost like a cartoon freeze-frame. It certainly held them off long enough for other officers to arrive and disperse them.'

Sunday, 28 June
Another long journey ahead, up to St Etienne for the second-round tie against Argentina. Plenty of time to discover how boring French radio can be; at least you can pick up Radio 5 Live in places.

Monday, 29 June
A briefing at St Etienne police station. Next to the rather bedraggled English spotters sit a smartly-uniformed three-man contingent from the Argentinian police. A French officer explains at length, with the aid of various charts, his plans for policing and segregation. Unfortunately he speaks entirely in French and none of the spotters understands a word.

Despite media reports suggesting an Argentinian hooligan threat, Eddie Curtis is unconcerned: 'They have 15 of what they call Category Cs, but we only call someone Category C if they actually direct problems. The Argentinians probably categorize people C if they cause trouble or are liable to follow trouble. So a very small number.'

The officers are then taken to the ground to have a look round, but the security staff refuse to let them in.

Tuesday, 30 June
The spotters hang around St Etienne police station for several hours waiting to be given instructions. While there, one of Huddersfield Town's best known 'boys' is brought in hand-cuffed. He banters with the spotters about their dress sense, proudly displaying his Burberry hat and Stone Island top.

St Etienne's police commander had promised to flood the streets with hundreds of armed officers and deal promptly with any troublemakers. Inevitably, some innocent fans are caught in the net and arrested. When they realize there are English police officers at the station they appeal for their help to get released.

Inevitably, many guilty parties escape arrest and at the

packed stadium that evening there are, for the first time at France 98, clashes inside a ground. Argentina's opening goal from a penalty is the trigger for a small disturbance behind the goal where the majority of English fans are gathered. Some try to cross the seats to attack rival fans. It is not long before similar trouble breaks out at the opposite end, where a small but vociferous number of English are in among the blue-and-white of their opponents.

Yet nothing in the stands is as dramatic as events on the pitch. For once, even the spotters find themselves watching the game more than the crowd.

England's exit sees a few scuffles at the ground and later in the town. Frustratingly for the spotters, three of those involved are Newcastle Category Cs who had earlier been pointed out to the French police, arrested but then released.

Wednesday, 1 July
A mixture of sadness and relief. All of the spotters, football fans themselves, wanted England to do well. But by now they are also tired and missing their families. Enough is enough.

With the pressure off, a game of soccer is organized against some local firemen. It is a time to unwind and, for Eddie Curtis, to look back at the past two-and-a-half weeks.

'It has gone very well. We had a strategy. We said we would point out the people who were liable to cause trouble, gather evidence on those who did cause trouble and advise the local police accordingly, and we did. The local police said they would deal with people swiftly and take them before the court, and they did. They said they would deal with them severely and give terms of imprisonment, and they did. Everybody has shown tremendous courage in some very difficult situations.'

The spotters themselves are left with indelible memories.

'It has been a marvellous experience, something I will never forget,' says one. 'Some of the situations we dealt with we have never had to deal with before. For example, I've been involved in disorder on a grand scale but never on such a scale as in Marseilles.'

For others, it is the end of an era. A third of the team who travelled to France are to leave soccer intelligence for other duties. Bill, after 15 years tracking headline-grabbing gangs, is on his way to a motorized beat in a rural English county. He admits that he might miss the hooligans.

'I think I will in a way. It has been a pleasure to stop them causing problems over the years. It'll be very difficult watching a football match after doing this job. If I go on my day off, I'll end up talking to people I know and not watching the game. Even when I watch it on TV, I look at the crowd – who's there? – I just can't help it. You become addicted.'

'Your Boys Took a Hell of a Beating'
How the FA Looked a Gift-horse in the Mouth

As a piece of television sports commentary the above quote is a classic up there with `They think it's all over'. For any England football fan who can remember the 1980s, England v Norway in Oslo, 9 September, 1981, is indelibly stamped on the memory. England lose to Norway for the first time – beaten 2-1 in the qualifying competition for the 1982 World Cup finals. As the final whistle goes, the Norwegian television commentator splutters into hysterical overdrive. A random litany of famous English names follows: 'Admiral Lord Nelson, Winston Churchill, Lady Diana'. Hoarse of voice and rapidly running out of famous English people to finger, he reaches a tremulous finale: 'Maggie Thatcher. Your boys took a hell of a beating!'

The obvious incredulity with which the result was greeted in Norway was also felt back home in England – minus the joy. England had been humiliated before in the international arena, but what made the defeat in Oslo so unacceptable to the hack-pack in Fleet Street was that Norway, as the newspapers at the time never tired of pointing out, were a nation of football part-timers.

Part-timers or not, by the 1990s their club sides had made something of a habit of upsetting the European ambitions of English Clubs. Manchester United were effectively put out of the 1994 Champions League by Gothenborg, Aston Villa were dismissed from the UEFA cup by Helsingborgs and Liverpool beaten in the same competition by Bronby.

It is true that only one Scandinavian club has ever lifted a European trophy (Gothenborg won the UEFA cup in 1982 and 1987) but ever since Alan Simonsen helped Borussia

Monchengladbach to UEFA Cup glory in 1975, Scandinavians have featured in many a conquering side, not least Manchester United, where Schmeichel, Solskjaer, Berg, Johnsen and Blomqvist all played their part in the record-breaking treble season.

Scandinavians can be found in numbers not only in our own leagues but also at top clubs all over Europe. Nor are these latter-day Vikings restricted to playing; coaches such as Sven Goran Eriksson, Sepp Piontek, Egil Olsen and Ebbe Skovdahl are respected and sought-after managers.

Despite this there are many in the English game who appear shocked and surprised when a Scandinavian team, club or country, puts one over on the English. Inevitably the post-match analysis tends to centre on how badly 'our boys' performed. Despite the growing number of Danes, Swedes and Norwegians in the Premier League (forty-five at the start of the 1998-99 season) the English do not seem to have asked themselves why Scandinavians have become such a force in world football.

It has certainly been no accident. Perhaps more galling, England – in at least two important respects – provided the inspiration behind this flowering of talent. Firstly through the screening of English football which has been shown on Scandinavian television since the 1960s. Secondly, it was the work of an English university sports scientist that inspired Bangsbo to write a key work that has informed the Scandinavian footballing renaissance. It was rejected by the English FA with the same disdain that our football writers habitually dismiss Scandic teams as part-timers.

This was puzzling and hurtful to those involved. Certainly ever since Scandinavian television began carrying *Match of the Day*, English football was an important inspiration to their foot-ballers and supporters. And, to this day, some of the biggest fan clubs for the likes of Manchester United, Liverpool and Arsenal can be found in Sweden, Norway and Denmark; clubs which easily outstrip their own domestic club fan base.

As recently as the 1980s Scandinavian sides knew exactly what to expect when they drew an English team in European competition. As Michael Shaffer, former Danish International and lately manager of FC Copenhagen, recalls: 'Then, from the players' and the managers' point of view, it was just an opportunity to cash a big cheque. No one believed that the Scandinavians would beat an English team.'

But times change and, by 1994, Jonas Brorsson and his team mates at Trelleborgs, a small town on the southern tip of Sweden, had their sights set a little higher than just a cheque when they drew Blackburn in the opening round of the UEFA Cup. Brorsson, at six-foot plus, is something of an identikit Scandinavian. He is a scheduling manager for a large international haulage firm based in Malmo and in his spare time, a centre-half.

Trelleborgs knew they had a job on their hands but crucially they were far from overawed at the prospect. A big fan of English club football, Brorsson had watched it on television for years. 'It is really entertaining to watch – very fast, very exciting. But it is also clear that when English footballers go abroad to play in European competition, sometimes they do not think very much.'

As far as the English press was concerned it was a forgone conclusion. Blackburn were on their way to the Premiership title, surely these Swedish minnows were a minor distraction to be suffered before the more substantial European challenges ahead. Alan Shearer was in blistering form, as was his striking partner Chris Sutton. Brorsson recalls that English journalists had only one line of questioning.

'All they talked about was how much money Shearer and Sutton were worth. They watched us train and after I had spoken with a journalist, he asked me what I thought our chances were? I said we could win. He just laughed and said "Shearer" to me. But I thought, well, you cannot play football with money. I think the English really underestimated us.'

Indeed they did. Trelleborgs beat Blackburn 1-0. Brorsson marked Shearer out of the game. The Swedish club completed the job a fortnight later drawing 2-2 at Ewood Park. As far as the English media was concerned the upset was the result of an appalling set of performances by the Premier League champions elect. No one paid much attention to Trelleborgs's achievement.

If the players and clubs were making their mark, so, increasingly in the 1990s, were the national sides. Denmark lifted the European championship in 1992, Norway made the World Cup finals for the first time in 1994, disposing of England along the way, while Sweden came third in USA 94 and handed out severe maulings to England in the 1992 and 2000 European Championship. By 1995 all three countries were ranked inside the top ten teams in the world. Yet the combined population of the three countries was only 17 million, a third of that in England.

As is often the case, the impetus to succeed is fuelled less by natural advantages and more by the need to combat handicaps. Chief among the factors hampering the development of a flourishing domestic football scene in Scandinavia was the climate.

In Sweden and Norway where the winters are long and severe, the league can only operate in the summer. The limited number of available match-days means the season is much shorter than in many other European countries, and because of this the football economy simply does not generate the kind of cash required to support a fully professional game in the respective leagues. In fact, in all of Scandinavia there are only five fully professional clubs: three in Denmark, two in Sweden and none at all in Norway.

A career in domestic football, therefore, was never really a viable choice for the average Scandinavian – and even less so in Denmark where payment was banned until 1978. Most clubs drew their players from universities or, more often than not, from young white-collar professionals in the early stages of their careers. But these players generally retired from the game by the time they were 28; and, even today, it is rare to find players, other than returnees, aged 30 or over, in domestic leagues.

But in the late 1960s the financial rewards on offer elsewhere in Europe, while hardly amounting to much compared with the amounts paid out today, began to rise. It was enough to tempt talented Scandinavian footballers to try their luck abroad.

The first to make an impact was Alan Simonsen crowned European Player of the Year in 1977. He helped Borussia Monchengladbach to a brace of UEFA Cup trophies and to a European Cup final (where they lost to Liverpool). But there were others such as Soren Lerby and Fran Arnesen, team mates of Johan Cruyff at Ajax.

However, soon after Denmark scrapped its amateur rule, the first generation of players and coaches, who had gone abroad to carve out their football careers, began to return home. Lars Bjeens, who works for the Danish FA, said: 'We have been able to get inspiration from outside our country because the players that we brought back to the national team playing in Spain, Italy, Germany and so on, brought back the best of foreign football to Denmark.'

One advantage of having a stunted football economy back home was that when the first generation of the foreign legion began to return they found few sacred-cow traditions and a domestic game eager to learn.

Inspired by the experiences of their returning professionals, the Scandinavian football clubs began building for success or, at the very least, changing the state of affairs whereby their clubs were on the receiving end of a severe thumping every time that the big guns from the English, Italian or Spanish leagues came calling. Mostly this was an informal process, although in Norway – shortly after their 1981 victory over England – the FA there set out a ten-year plan for success.

Crucially the process involved more than cherry-picking tactics and playing systems. Given that domestic players were overwhelmingly part-time and training opportunities at a premium, coaches had every motivation to seek out the most effective and cutting-edge methods of player preparation. Their sport scientists started looking around to see what they could find. What they discovered surprised them.

At a number of Scandinavian universities and research institutes sport science had been an established discipline for some years. Physiologists, notably Professor Bjorn Ekblom at the

Karolinska Institute, were researching fitness in a whole range of sports, especially athletics, tennis and the popular Scandinavian pursuits of orienteering and cross-country skiing.

Technical directors and coaches in a variety of mainly Olympic sports were very interested in this kind of research because, especially in athletics, it was realized that, at least in the case of European men, the limits of human performance were close to being reached and that any improvements in performance would have to be eked out of scientific advances in fitness-and-training methods.

But when the football coaches came knocking they drew a blank. In football, it appeared, fitness-training techniques had changed little in 50 years. Even the returning exiles reported that fitness-training abroad was not so different from home, except, as professionals, they could devote more time to it. As Ebbe Skovdahl, now manager at Aberdeen but for many years coach at the Bronby club in Copenhagen, put it: 'What we needed in Denmark were some books that were related to football, not to athletics – running or jumping or whatever.'

Fortunately for Ebbe Skovdahl, these were questions that physiologists at Stockholm's Karolinska Institute and the University of Copenhagen's August Krogh Institute, which were appalled at the lack of work on fitness in the world's biggest sport, were beginning to address. Physiologists like Professor Jens Bangsbo, for example, had a fairly uncomplicated view on how the performance of soccer players might be improved. 'Football is not a science,' he said, 'but there is no doubt that science can improve football.'

This may sound like a statement of the obvious but, as recently as 1987, when Bangsbo uttered these words, it was radical talk. The initial search for any application of sports science in football had led, irony of ironies, to England.

The first full-time England manager, Walter Winterbottom, published what is believed to be the first modern tome on fitness in professional football in 1959. It was fairly rudimentary, but in essence the questions that it asked were much the same as those being asked by people at the cutting edge of the discipline today.

Winterbottom wanted to know just how much energy footballers expended while playing a game.

He decided to do this by measuring the distance covered by players during a game. He found that the average was around five miles, although this varied depending on position in the team. Winterbottom, inspired by this discovery, made sure all his players could run comfortably non-stop for the length of time that their position dictated. Much later, others in England – notably Professor Tom Riley of John Moores University in Liverpool – picked up this particular baton of knowledge and ran with it.

'I started work at Liverpool Polytechnic (now John Moores University) in 1972. My research into what sport science could do for football, drawing on validated scientific data published in 1976, culminated in the first paper on the subject in this country.'

Professor Riley had managed to persuade a football club to allow him to collect this data. You might believe the club would be proud to trumpet its progressive attitude, and certainly in any other sport it would have been grounds for cranking the publicity machine into overdrive. But this was football and the club was more concerned it would become a laughing stock among its peers. To this day Tom Riley has never revealed its identity.

Whereas Walter Winterbottom had simply used external observation to support his conclusions, Riley went beyond these simplistic subjective methods and, using validated scientific data-collection protocols, measured the heart rate, oxygen intake and muscle mass of players during various states of training matches.

If he had expected that English football managers would soon be beating a path to his door to discover what his work could do for their players he was disappointed. 'Being a scientist and working in football was very, very hard work. I met a lot of resistance because there were so few enlightened managers.'

In 1979, he wrote a book entitled *What Research Tells the Coach About Soccer*. Aware that football coaches in England had no interest in what science could tell them, he published it in the

United States instead. 'There was not much point in putting it out in the UK. It would only have sold half-a-dozen copies. The Americans were much more interested in sports science in general and it did quite well over there.'

In simple terms, what people like Tom Riley were telling coaches who were prepared to listen was that football is an intermittent type of exercise where short periods of high-intensity exercise are randomly interspersed with longer periods of either active or passive recovery. Training needed to be tailored accordingly. Players needed to be both aerobically fit, i.e., able to run long distances, and anaerobically fit, i.e., able to produce great bursts of power at any given point in the game, especially in the final third when statistically most games are decided. Riley advocated what is known as interval training techniques to achieve this happy state.

But his work fell on deaf ears. His principal 'crime' as far as the English footballing establishment was concerned, was that he had never played professional football and, therefore, could not possibly have anything useful to pass on. His work remained of only academic interest until about five years ago when Everton and Liverpool began to look at the expertise in these areas. He is currently working with top professionals like Michael Owen on further research into bio-mechanics in football.

Ignored in the land whose taxpayers funded his research, Professor Riley became much admired abroad – especially in Scandinavia where, in the middle 1980s, his work provided inspiration for a number of sports scientists and physiologists, like Professor Bangsbo, who were interested in sport science and football. Meanwhile in England, the philosophy of football fitness training, if you can call it that, never got much beyond Winterbottom.

Fitness for generations of English managers became equated with the ability to run long distances – a belief additionally inspired by the large number of military PT instructors freelancing their wares in sport. But it appears not to have occurred to many in the game that preparing a soldier to trek miles over rough terrain was a different matter to preparing a footballer for a 90-minute match.

By 1985 a number of universities and higher education institutes in this country had begun to fund research into sport science and offer it as an undergraduate course. One such college was the South Glamorgan Institute of Higher Education where Paul Bolsom, an occasional youth player with Torquay United, was a student. He achieved a BA before going off to complete a Masters in Sport Science at an American University.

On his return to England in 1989, armed with considerable knowledge about such matters as interval training, he contacted some football clubs to see if there was a market for his services. 'I went to a club, which I will not name, and asked what sort of things they did to improve fitness. The answer was: "As a manager, I have played for 30 years, my physiotherapist has played for 30 years and my assistant trainer has played for 30 years. We do not need any more experience."'

Bolsom found this attitude to be almost universal within the English game and, like Professor Riley, took his expertise elsewhere. In his case he found work at the Karolinska Institute, Stockholm, where he specialized in the physiology of football players. He is now a full-time physiologist with the Swedish FA. So, an Englishman who, as recently as 1989, was not given the time of day by English football clubs, is now applying his knowledge to building an ever expanding canon of knowledge for one of our international rivals. It gets worse.

In 1988 Jens Bangsbo, inspired by Professor Riley's work, began producing the first of a series of pamphlets on applied science in football. Just as Professor Riley had done, he concentrated on the mysteries of interval training. On the surface it was pretty dry stuff, guaranteed in its raw state to baffle football folk in any country. But Bangsbo was a rare creature, a scientist who had played football to a high level, representing Denmark in the Olympic games at a time when the Olympic team was the pinnacle of the game in that country.

With almost unlimited access to footballers because he was still playing himself when he began his work, he was in a position to pursue more sophisticated research than his predecessors in the field. 'At first I was able to use the players on my team and myself as subjects in my study. And as some of these players had good connections with other teams, I was able to contact them and ask them if they were interested in my studies.'

Certainly technology was also on his side. One of the most accurate indicators of physical fitness is heart rate, and, while Riley had to rely on breathing machines attached to players while they ran around, which is hardly conducive to normal play, Bangsbo was able to strap more discreet heart monitors to his players. Then, as time and technology progressed, he was also able to download to a computer an individual player's second-by-second fitness and performance profile during a match.

He also videotaped training sessions and analyzed motion characteristics of footballers in action, reasoning that if football taxed some muscles more than others, he wanted to find out which ones and how best these could be exercised and prepared to avoid injury or burn-out.

'In some cases I tested players on Wednesday and played against them on Sunday, but they were very willing to do these type of things because they saw a possibility for developing into better footballers.'

Bangsbo began to experiment with new training and fitness techniques and was then able to measure their suitability for footballers. His contacts put him in touch with top Danish side Brönby and Ebbe Skovdahl.

Skovdahl, keen to have answers to the questions that Bangsbo was asking, invited him to work with the Brönby team. No one – least of all Ebbe Skovdahl – thought there was anything especially radical about admitting a physiologist to their midst. 'Of course, I was interested in having a scientist who wanted to go into the best thing to do when training football players.'

Bangsbo used Brönby as a human laboratory in which to build detailed research into the nature of fitness in football. One of the crucial fitness elements of the game, he discovered, was that players spent remarkably little time expending high energy. For example, in a second-by-second tracking of Sweden's forward Martin Dahlin in a ten-minute period during a World Cup game, it was found that Dahlin had possession of the ball for just seven seconds, sprinted for nine seconds, ran at high speed for thirty-six seconds, jogged for three minutes and seven seconds and spent the other six minutes or so standing still or walking.

All this data, however interesting, was not much use if the coaches could not apply it to their players. It also became clear that although the incidence of high levels of speed during a game were few and far between, they were generally instrumental in determining the path of the ball and thus ultimately the fate of the game.

Bangsbo concluded that the best training should always involve a football since this not only conditioned a player in the best way, but also helped the player to improve his technique. With the help of top-flight coaches he then designed training routines that addressed the twin imperatives of maximum fitness with optimum ball control. Among those at Brönby at the time who would be familiar to English football fans were Peter Schmiechel (Manchester United) and Mark Rieper (West Ham and Celtic).

In 1989, he published his scientific papers in a user-friendly, generously illustrated book entitled *Fitness Training in Football: A Scientific Approach*. The book explained the physiology of football in simple terms and went on to extrapolate coaching methods and training techniques that would help get the best out of a footballer.

It was especially appropriate to Scandinavia because, by combining fitness and technique in the same exercises, it delivered more than the traditional coach's approach to pre-play preparation in less time. It was a message that Scandinavia's part-time footballers wanted to hear. They may have limited time, but now they had the means to make the best use of it. The Danish Football Association was so impressed it immediately dispatched the book to every club in the country.

'Because of the Danish FA's endorsement and involvement, the book spread pretty fast,' Bangsbo recalls. 'It was also used in the education system. It was the same story in Sweden where the work was translated.'

Professor Bangsbo's book is not, of course, a blue-print for world domination in football. No book could be that. As Ebbe Skovdahl says: 'It is not a bible'. Success in sport is never that easy to achieve. The magic of football – or indeed any sport – is that winners are forged from an uncertain alchemy of talent, fortune, coaching and motivation. What the book can do is deliver a cutting edge to a team that absorbs the basic principles of what it has to say rather than sticking with more laborious less effective training methods. As Skvodahl says: 'Jens Bangsbo is a clever guy with some good ideas who knows what he is talking about. Almost every coach in Denmark who is serious about football has the book'.

Fitness Training in Football became very popular with coaches and players alike in Scandinavia because its exercises are self-evidently relevant, and had an air of common sense about them. For example, consider these extracts:

After cessation of exercise, the temperature of the previously activated muscles decreases quickly and is back to the pre-exercised level after 15 minutes. A warm up before a match should therefore continue until the start of the match. In top class football the players often return to the dressing room for 15 minutes and stay there. During this time the benefit of the warm up is lost. (On this point Brönby provoked much comment when it was to play Liverpool at Anfield in the UEFA Cup. It set up a mini five-a-side game which carried on almost to the whistle for the start of the game.)

Speed training should mainly take the form of game-like situations since part of the desired training effect is to improve the players ability to anticipate and react in football. Sprinting a set distance on a given command has little effect on the ability to react in football specific situations.

With a state-of-the-art fitness reference book underpinning a keen desire to study and improve technical and tactical knowledge, players responded with enthusiasm to the new regimes. In quite a short period of time the work of Bangsbo, and others, indeed the whole system of coaching and player preparation in Scandinavia, was overhauled.

Take Jonas Brorsson's training schedule at Trelleborgs. 'We train four times a week. We have the longest pre-season in the world – January to April. We have, for example, one-day indoor training when we just concentrate on technique, then a day of tactical training. We each keep a fitness diary in which we enter everything we do or eat.'

Across the water in Copenhagen, Michael Shaffer ran through the FC Copenhagen training schedule: 'We train every afternoon at about two o'clock, and at ten in the morning on Wednesdays, so that is five sessions a week. We have an hour's session on Saturday and play on Sunday. Then some of the players get together one morning during the week to work on specific routines related to their position in the team'.

In stark contrast to that regime, it may be a shock for you to learn that, on average, a Premier League player trains four mornings a week, for about two hours; and a lot less if there is a mid-week match. That is about the same as Jonas Brorsson at Trelleborgs without the hassle of keeping a fitness diary, and some five hours less than the professionals at Copenhagen. Yet Brorsson and his like are still branded as part-timers.

It is only legitimate to point out that English clubs have many more matches, a longer season, and games that tend to be more physically intense and competitive. Certainly Howard Wilkinson, the English FA's technical director, but former manager of Leeds United and Sheffield Wednesday, believes that given the demands of the English game it is impossible to keep players at peak fitness for any length of time.

'The players undergo a crazy programme here. It is impossible to get players to peak twice a week and for as many times as we would want them to. So we finish up fudging, finish up making the best of a bad job – making do.'

In Wilkinson's view, the short pre-season in England does not help either: 'Players are fitter two weeks before the start of the season than they are at any time during the season. I know there is an old football saying that your fitness will improve as you get match-fit, but in my opinion that's clap-trap.'

Paul Bolsom thinks that it is clap-trap, too: 'It is perfectly possible to design training programmes to suit – whatever your playing schedule. That is the whole point of interval training. It addresses the problem of recovery.'

English football has always been inward looking. With so few people who speak Swedish or Danish at the English FA, the work of Bangsbo – and others in Scandinavia – could have slipped by unnoticed. But Bangsbo offered the English FA all his knowledge on a plate, and, by association, the work of many other physiologists and sports scientists at work in Scandinavia.

In 1990 he was a visiting professor at Loughborough University's department of sport science and physical education. Its head was – and at the time of writing is – Professor Clyde Williams. Williams excitedly brought Bangsbo's work to the attention of Charles Hughes who was then technical director of the English Football Association. Williams suggested that such a book might be a welcome addition to the F.A.'s lexicon of coaching. Hughes, about to publish his own controversial work, *The Winning Formula,* remarked that the FA was to publish its own work on such matters.

Reflecting back, Bangsbo is unclear if Hughes meant that *The Winning Formula* would cover the ground laid down in Bangsbo's own, or if the FA was planning to produce one. What is clear, however, is that no book equating to Bangsbo's work emerged from Lancaster Gate.

Certainly the thrust of Hughes's book, *The Winning Formula,* had little to do with player preparation, its concern was tactical and, somewhat unfairly, it has come to be seen as the long-ball bible. At least the book was based on exhaustive research. After analyzing 25 years of goals stored in the FA's video and film library, Hughes found that the vast majority were scored after five passes or fewer. Hence the quicker the ball is moved from your own goal area to your opponent's the more goals you are likely to score.

Whatever the value of *The Winning Formula,* it certainly was not a competitor to Bangsbo or any other Scandinavian physiologist's work. Either way, the English FA decided it had no need for Bangsbo's book.

One nation that embraced both philosophies was Norway where former national coach Egil Olsen (now with Wimbledon), a keen advocate of *The Winning Formula,* was also publicly scathing about the fitness conditioning of players in the English League. In the year before France 98, he went as far to say he wished his top players would choose other countries in which to ply their trade.

In 1994, with the help of the Danish Football Association, Bangsbo published an English edition of his book, and once again tried to interest the English footballing establishment in his work. Once again he was ignored. 'When the English edition was published I sent it to the English FA, but I do not think I ever heard from them. I am, of course, very happy when anyone finds value in my work so I was disappointed by their lack of response.'

Lars Bjeens of the Danish FA was likewise disappointed, but not surprised: 'I love English football and Derby County has been my team since the early 1970s. There has been some dream football in the Premier League and some outstanding goals. The only problem is that England has been isolated from the Continent for years. The attitude in England is that the game was born here and we know how to play. You have not really looked at how football has developed in other parts of the world.'

In the rest of the footballing world, however, the response to Bangsbo's book was more enthusiastic. It has been translated into French, Spanish, Italian, Greek, Turkish, German and Arabic, and is a standard textbook on coaching for dozens of football associations around the world.

In the last couple of seasons there has been some indication that English clubs are finally taking a more scientific approach to football fitness. At Arsenal, for example, the likes of Martin Keown and Tony Adams have spoken frequently – and almost in awe – of the benefit of stretching; and many Premier League players have radically changed their diet, or discovered the benefits of warming down after training and games.

But Paul Bolsom believes there is still a long way to go:

'Obviously a fair number of our national squad players play in England and, when I ask them about English training routines, etc., they mostly shake their heads in despair. So, yes, one or two managers might have imported some of the more enlightened regimes but for the most part the preparation of footballers in England is still in the dark ages.'

Arsenal, Manchester United and Chelsea, however, are ahead of the game. At Manchester United, for example, Brian Kidd and Steve McClaren, his successor as first-team coach, are both regular visitors to European clubs where they study training and coaching techniques first hand.

But stray much beyond a handful of Premier League clubs and you will find that the majority of managers and coaches have no relevant qualifications and are, as likely as not, stitching together a training and coaching culture based on hearsay and their own experiences as players.

There is little incentive to seek out new techniques and training methods, or the latest information on the preparation of players, if you do not need any qualifications to get a job in the first place.

By contrast, Paul Bolsom says that in Sweden there is a hunger for knowledge among coaches at all levels. But then to coach at any level in Sweden you need the relevant Swedish FA-sanctioned qualification. 'When we (the Swedish FA) lay on weekend coaching seminars they are packed – 200 coaches is not unusual. And the people are not there for the junketing; they get down to the work on Friday night and keep at it full pelt, eight hours a day with minimum breaks on a Saturday and Sunday. There are only 14 teams in our top division, so these people must be coaching at all levels of football and going back home armed with the very latest knowledge.'

Brandishing such cutting-edge enthusiasm and thinking in English football – especially outside the Premier League – would probably be seen as a positive disadvantage for any coach hoping to find employment. English football clubs are, by nature, suspicious of anything that challenges accepted practice and, even if the board did buy it, the likelihood is that the players would not.

John Brewer, is the head of the Human Performance Centre at the Lilleshall National Sports Centre. He was part of the medical team that accompanied the England squad to the World Cup in 1990. 'Player power,' he says, 'still dominates the culture of most football clubs – and what the players want to do in terms of training or eating is what tends to happen. Managers might try and change a diet or routine, but if the players are not happy with that it tends not to last very long; and if the change is not an instant success then quite often they will revert back to their own tried-and-tested techniques.'

Howard Wilkinson, the FA's Technical Director, agrees with him. Even in his latter years at Leeds, he says, it was a struggle, when it came to changing familiar methods and routines, to win the hearts and minds of all his players. 'English players are always very reluctant to be seen taking things seriously. An Italian footballer prides himself on being seen to take his job seriously, but we are embarrassed by that.'

At the start of the 1998-99 season there were 38 Danish, Swedish and Norwegians playing in the Premier League, and this number had risen to 45 by the end of the season. The appearance of so many Scandinavians in our leagues is generally explained away on the grounds that they are cheaper to acquire than a like-for-like English player. While this is doubtless true, it is also true that they have earned their places in Premier League teams on merit. They train better, and have better technique and tactical awareness than many of our own home-grown players.

In 1995 Howard Wilkinson, then at Leeds United, said the only hope for English football was to recognize that we had much to learn about preparing players for professional football. 'Denmark, Norway, Sweden, even Germany and, going back ten years, France, have almost sat down and said let's forget what has gone before, let's start again. What is it we are after? What do we want to do? They have had a campaign. We need a campaign.'

Five years later he is, of course, in a position to conduct such a campaign and, with the creation of football academies and training protocols for juniors, is showing signs that he means to do just that. (There is an appraisal of both these initiatives in chapters eight and nine of this book.) Maybe in five years' time, even if Bangsbo and his ilk remain largely unknown on these shores, what they have to tell us about football fitness and player preparation will not.

CHAPTER SEVEN

Grounds for Concern
The Dreadful Pitches That Injure Hundreds a Year

Unless you play in the Stockton and District League Division Three, you have probably never heard of Paul Gibson. But if you've ever played football on a pitch you thought wasn't up to scratch, then his story is one you will be familiar with. A 26-year-old Middlesborough-based financial advisor, Paul was captain of his work's Sunday team. His story is one of an horrific accident – an accident which is becoming more and more common, a trend that is causing painful injuries to footballers and alarm among councillors, lawyers, insurance brokers and groundsmen. It's also a trend which could – and should – have been reversed nearly 20 years ago.

As soon as his team mates saw Paul Gibson intercept the opposition's through-ball, they knew the danger was over and they could relax. The central defender calmly took the ball under his control, then, turning away from goal and ignoring the calls to hoof it aimlessly into space, broke from defence himself. It was when he charged across the halfway line that the most dramatic event of his footballing career happened.

'The centre forward caught me from behind and I fell,' Gibson said recalling his fateful break from defence. 'I clenched my ankle, but when I turned and saw my knee there was a three- or four-inch cut right across the kneecap. You could actually see the kneecap.'

Paul bears no malice towards the centre forward. It's a contact sport and as far as Paul is concerned the occasional trip is all part of the game. What happened to his knee wasn't, in his view, either players' fault. It is the pitch that Paul blames for his torment. He's taking legal action against the local council for providing what he claims is a dangerous surface to play on, and is suing his local football association because, he says, the referee should have stopped the match before his injury. Both the accused bodies deny responsibility.

'It was the normal kind of council pitch you play on every Sunday morning. However, there was very little grass around the halfway line and it was in that area that I fell. We were playing the week before Christmas 1997, the last game before the Christmas break. Halfway through the first half, a team mate of mine cut his knee when he fell. It was only a small cut, but he needed to go to hospital for stitches. The referee checked the area where he fell and allowed the game to continue.'

It was mid-way through the second half, while his team mate was still waiting at the casualty department, that Paul's kneecap made its unwelcome and gory appearance. Players from both teams gathered around him in the centre-circle, amazed that such an ordinary looking tumble could result in such a fleshy mess. He, too, was whisked off to hospital, still in his football kit. Sweaty, muddied and bloodied, he joined the accident and emergency queue.

'My wound was stitched up by the doctor, inside and out. They gave me various tetanus injections, a course of antibiotics and sent me home.' But the agony didn't end there. 'I spent all week in bed, I couldn't move. I was on quite strong pain killers, but was still in pain and, even a week later, the swelling hadn't gone down. I was still using an ice pack, still not moving and still off work.' A week after the first consultation, Paul returned to have his stitches removed. It was a routine appointment for one o'clock, but by three o'clock he was having emergency surgery and in the following week he required two more operations.

'I've been diagnosed as having septic arthritis,' he explains. 'Six months after the tackle, the infection in my kneecap was so bad that it had spread into the bone. I've gone through the worst pain of my life and any chance of me playing contact sport again is very small.'

Now Paul has to spend the weekends watching his friends from the touchline. He admits that he's not much of a spectator:

'I work from nine 'til five, Monday to Friday, sometimes later. The weekend is the one time when I can enjoy myself, but now I've lost the one thing I love doing most.'

Blaming pitches for causing injuries is now becoming increasingly common. Week after week amateur soccer players are having their footballing careers destroyed by sub-standard surfaces.

More than a thousand cases are recorded every year by the government's Leisure Accident Surveillance System which collects reports from hospital casualty departments; and up and down the country doctors are confronted by scores of patients with stories to tell of uneven pitches, pot-holes in the ground and rocks in the grass.

'The patient sprained his knee joint after falling down a pot-hole while playing football' reports one doctor. 'The 20-year-old patient was running for a ball when he fell in a hole and twisted his ankle,' notes another. Such records are typical, and most of the accidents happen on sports facilities provided by local councils.

Jean Wengar, of the National Playing Fields Association, is not surprised by the number of complaints. 'Certainly we're aware of pitches that are unsafe, pitches where rabbits are digging up the ground and matches are being cancelled,' he says. 'Pitches are of depleting quality. Fifteen to twenty years ago pitches lasted far longer, had less muddy goalmouths and were overall of better quality.'

Where facilities are unsafe, players can – and often do – follow the route taken by Paul Gibson and sue. There are no reliable figures for the number of bad-pitch compensation claims, but estimates put the number at around a dozen in recent years and everyone involved in the industry knows of a litigation or two.

As Sport and Landscape Consultant with Nottinghamshire County Council, Steve Thomas knows of a number of court cases. 'It's becoming something of a growth industry,' he says with obvious regret. 'In some instances, people are looking for a reason to take other people to court and this is something of great concern to local authorities.'

What the courts are being asked to determine is whether or not councils are providing unsafe surfaces for soccer. Where Steve Thomas comes into the picture is as an expert witness. Armed with a trowel, knife and bag of assorted tricks, he has visited many pitches where players claim they have suffered injuries. 'I've seen some poor quality pitches where the drainage is bad, where the ground is uneven or where there are sharp stones poking through the topsoil. I've also seen some exceptionally bad pitches which have definitely been unsafe to play on.'

Such symptoms of sportsfield malaise are only too familiar to thousands of weekend amateurs all over the country. The cliché is to call these players the grass roots of football, but given the lack of greensward that many of them are forced to play on it's an inappropriate pun. The quality of some of the pitches is so low that many matches are wrecked by bobbles, puddles, ruts and molehills; and some pitches are dangerous.

The grey area between what is, and what is not, quantifiably dangerous has allowed lawyers to develop a new sport of their own. They spend months, even years, arguing whether this or that pitch is dangerous or just sub-standard; and while they debate the finer points of topsoil distribution, more players are ending up in casualty.

Into this sorry state of soccer affairs stepped an unlikely looking saviour – a pitch doctor with a mission.

Under cloudy spring skies, a man in his sixties, with a shock of white hair and the deep tan of a person with an outdoor life, is stripped to the waist and lying motionless on the grass. This is Peter Dury and he is busy. As balls drop one by one from a purpose-built metal frame on to the sportsfield, Peter records how high they bounce. He has the answer to the pitch problem, but unfortunately it came nearly 40 years too late for his own benefit.

'I had to finish playing amateur football when I was 27. I went up for a header and when I came down my foot landed in a pot-hole and I tore the ligaments in my ankle.' Peter tried to resume his career four times, but on each occasion his ligaments went again. Now, during the winter months, he suffers from severe pains in his ankle. 'If it hadn't been for that pot-hole, I could have played for many more years and been free from all this pain. Today, people would probably take out a compensation claim against the council, but in those days you just put up with it.'

Unable to play, Peter Dury devoted his life to the art of groundsmanship. He was responsible for the new pitches at Anfield, Highbury and Villa Park and has been used as a consultant at countless other top venues. But football is most in his debt for his work on the country's parks' pitches.

The principle is simple: if it is possible to set standards for measuring the quality of hotels, then it must be possible to set standards for measuring the quality of pitches. It was with this logical approach in mind that Peter Dury started work, with the help of Arthur Dye at the Sports Council. 'We began in the early seventies,' remembers Mr Dye, 'largely because of the rapid growth in artificial pitches which were being used as a substitute for natural grass.'

Like the haunting recollection of an embarrassing romance, or a photograph taken from a decade that fashion forgot, artificial pitches hold an unenviable position in footballing memories. Queens Park Rangers paid £350,000 for the first green carpet in professional soccer in the summer of 1981, and Luton, Oldham and Preston North End soon did the same.

If you hated mud, lawn-mowers and pot-holes, then artificial grass seemed to be a good idea, but the price was third-degree carpet burns, outrageous bounce and a new pair of specially soled trainers. Only the most chronic of hay-fever sufferers could think that the pros outweighed the cons.

Of course, plastic-grass technology has improved enormously, but when it first started there were tremendous problems. Some places installed a substance which seemed to have been stolen from the window display of a greengrocer's shop. Edges frayed, joins lifted and holes appeared. Industry standards had to be set – a sort of kite mark for fake grass. Once that had been established things started to improve – although not fast enough for the football league. Within seven years of being laid, the carpets at QPR, Luton, Preston and Oldham had all been ripped up.

It was the process of kite-marking synthetic grass carpets that led Dury and Dye to try and solve the problems of deteriorating parks' pitches. 'Once we had identified the qualities that were needed for synthetic surfaces,' said Mr Dye, 'we could identify the appropriate qualities we wanted to find on real grass.'

Throughout the 1970s to the 1980s Peter Dury got his hands dirty putting into practice what Arthur Dye championed in the Sports Council. Using his by now vast experience of pitch preparation, he created a list of easily understood criteria which could be used to measure the quality of any piece of grass for a sporting purpose. The criteria were then applied by council groundsmen to ensure that they concentrated their work on the pitches that needed it, and did not waste effort on grounds that were already up to scratch.

Ball roll, bounce, depth of soil, length of grass and evenness of surface are the components of a good soccer pitch, and now, thanks to Peter Dury, they can all be measured. 'You can save money by testing,' says the groundsmans' guru. 'It's just like going to the doctors to have a check-up. Having examined your body, he tells you where your weaknesses are – tells you to do this and not that. We do the same for sports pitches. It gives us the opportunity to put faults right without having to waste money. We're not guessing; we know what the faults are.'

Peter's work, outlining three levels of quality for pitches – basic, standard and high – is to be published by the Institute of Groundsmanship (I.O.G.). The criteria are so simple that one wonders why nobody drew up such tests before. The answer is that they could have been introduced long ago, but political dogma and bureaucracy prevented them from being applied and, at the same time, allowed more pitches to become unsafe.

This occurred because the period of research into pitch technology coincided with a major change in the way that sports pitches were managed. It was the 1980s and the Thatcherite privatization policy meant that local authorities, which had always used their own staff to care for parks, now had to make the work available to private contractors. Compulsory Competitive Tendering (CCT), in fact, had a bigger impact on grass-roots football than anything the FA or FIFA ever came up with.

'It's been a dead weight around the construction and maintenance of pitches,' asserts Jean Wengar of the National Playing Fields Association. 'While in theory it [CCT] should work properly, in practice it involves too many people with too much disparate knowledge to inspect pitches and ensure they are maintained properly. We're aware of situations where 13 people have been wandering around a site, scratching their heads, trying to work out what's wrong with a pitch.'

The years of expertise that had been built up in council parks' departments and embodied in a small number of experienced groundsmen was sacrificed for compulsory privatization.

In theory, CCT should have meant better, safer pitches for everyone as councils opened up the groundsman's shed to specialist contractors with expert, green-fingered, employees; and it should have saved money as bright, young entrepreneurs competed with each other to offer the lowest price. But the reason CCT had the opposite effect is because of the way that councils drew up the contracts.

The leisure officer at Bexley Council, Kent, is Colin Cannon, one of a progressive breed of local government officers. He has seen at first hand how daft the contract system can be, and the disastrous effects it can have on soccer matches. 'The original deals under CCT were let on what were called *input* contracts. These specified to the contractor when, what and how things had to be done. For example, you could specify that the grass had to be cut on *x* number of occasions throughout the cutting season and that's what would be done. The problems came if we had a wet, warm spring and the grass grew faster, then the contractors would want extra payments for the extra work to keep the grass short.

'Everything was done by job ticket. The council would issue a job ticket for every item of work that needed doing. It created a situation with the contractors' employees where they wouldn't do anything unless they had a ticket in their hand.'

Mow it on Monday, regardless of how long the grass is; water it on Wednesday, no matter how much rain there has been.

This kind of jobsworth approach to pitch preparation made it inevitable that pitches would become dangerous. Councils did not need a qualified groundsman, all they required was a YTS lad, a lawnmower and a calendar.

Peter Dury has a stack of stories about how the policy worked in practice. 'I was at a local authority depot one day when I overheard the foreman shout to the bloke driving the tractor "Cut it as close as you can, Bill, then we won't have to do the bugger for the rest of the year". It was ludicrous – the whole point of looking after a football pitch is not to strip it bare, but to make sure the grass on it is at the right height.'

So, while the privatization policy was busily butchering football facilities, Peter Dury pressed ahead with his pioneering standards, getting closer every season to developing what he called *Performance Quality Standards* for grass pitches. His only problem was that as he worked, things were getting worse. 'One local authority pitch was built on a bed of flint stones. The flints kept coming up through the surface and one player gashed his leg. The wound turned septic and he ended up having to have an operation. Now he walks with a limp.'

When this case came before the judge, Peter was called as an expert witness. 'It was desperately sad – should never have happened. That pitch should never have been played on.'

'Obviously this kind of thing is of great concern to us,' says Pat Gosset, from the offices of his Institute of Groundsmanship. 'The whole ethos of the I.O.G. is one which tries to protect the standards of groundsmanship and to get recognition for the status of the profession. The changes that took place under local authority contracts certainly didn't do us any favours as far as the quality of sports grounds is concerned.'

The situation has not only led to councils being sued by footballers, but the councils suing their contractors. The contractors then respond by producing a job sheet covered in ticked-off checkpoints and point out that they have mowed, watered and rolled the required number of times. Thus the disputes are sucked into a vortex of contractual litigation which benefits nobody but the lawyers.

All the time while this was going on, Peter Dury and the Sports Council had the answer to everybody's problems. However, just when they could have been beating a path to the printers to get their *Performance Quality Standards* published, Dury was forced to delay. 'We didn't publish because we wanted people to substantiate that the benchmarks we were setting were the right ones.'

In 1982 the standards were finally ready to be published. For the first time people could have known how to test and prepare pitches; and even the most clueless tractor driver could have worked out for himself if the grass needed cutting, rolling, watering or forking.

Instead, it was decided to keep the information within the scientific community. The Sports Council held back in the hope of convincing the British Standards Authority to back the *Performance Quality Standards*. If that support could be gained, the standards would carry greater legal weight. As Arthur Dye explains, 'It was largely because we wanted to see the standards we had been working on translated into mandatory British standards. What we had done in the past was produce our own ideas which could only be advisory, so we decided to extend the process one stage further and go for a standard that would be accepted nationally.'

Tragically, the road to publication was lengthened by a tortuous detour which has twisted through every European country and led to an impenetrable maze of international bureaucracy.

A top groundsmen is a canny character with knowledge of how a living sward will develop over time. But even the most proficient forecaster could not have foreseen that something as seemingly irrelevant as the Maastricht Treaty would scupper the planned improvements to our soccer pitches. It dictated that no member of European Union could develop its own standards for pitches, unless those standards were uniformly accepted by every other member.

'We were aware that there were movements across Europe to try to rationalize standards that had been developed in other countries,' explains Mr Dye, 'so, again, we saw this as an opportunity to develop a wider European formal process which, hopefully, would have a wider level of authority and agreement.'

What started as a bright and practical idea on the football pitches of Peter Dury's native Nottinghamshire, has become nothing more than another discussion point for committees of Eurocrats. While bleeding and bruised soccer players hobble from park pitches to hospitals, they are doubtless encouraged that civil servants are touring the Continent trying to assess the international uniformity of topsoil. And the best estimates are that this particularly gravy train will chug along until at least 2003 before a decision on the correct level of Euro-standards will be agreed.

To make matters worse, the Sports Council, which had been backing the process from the start, pulled out. 'It was disastrous, absolutely disastrous,' says Jean Wengar of the National Playing Fields Association. 'Up until then the Sports Council had supported the research but, when it pulled the rug, the standards work effectively frittered away. We're now left with a holding exercise to try to ensure that the Europeans take on board as much of the UK perspective as possible. We're at a tremendous disadvantage compared to other countries.'

Why would the Sports Council (now Sport England) pull out of supporting research which will make sport safer for everyone who competes on grass? Arthur Dye is defensive: 'One of our principal ways of working is to pump-prime and we thought we had primed this pump for quite long enough, and the impetus was there for the people we had worked with to finish the exercise. I had every confidence that they were well on the way to achieving the standards we had all been working for.'

But without the input of the Sports Council to hold all the parts together, the work fractured into splinter groups. The I.O.G. decided to ignore the politicians and prepare what they had for publication, while another influential body, the Sports Turf Research Institute (STRI), chose to wait until everyone else in Europe is ready.

Nestling alongside a beautiful parkland golf course in Bingley, West Yorkshire, the STRI has more knowledge about sports surfaces than can be found anywhere else in the UK, if not Europe. Just as a good waiter knows which wine goes with every item on the menu, the STRI officers, who have played a vital part in putting crucial scientific data into Peter Dury's findings, know which mix of grass seed suits each blend of soil.

'The STRI has done an enormous amount of research work starting in 1983, looking at the performance requirement of various pitches,' claims Dr Steven Baker from his office in stable buildings next to the clubhouse. But, he adds, the research will remain with the STRI until the European consultation period has run its full course. 'I head the UK delegation on the European standards and I think it will be confusing if two sets of standards are produced. In many respects we will be better off waiting for the European standards to come out because these will have much more force than those being developed by the IOG.' Pat Gosset of the IOG disagrees: 'We're more than pleased that the STRI are working on European standards, but there is also a need at the present time for standards which can be implemented and used immediately. Like many things, you can't wait forever.'

With this lack of unity from the scientists, it is not surprising that the most forward looking of councils has lost patience and decided to go it alone. After years of witnessing decline in the parks that he is responsible for, Colin Cannon at Bexley ripped up the input style contracts he had with the companies who looked after the pitches and used Peter Dury's work to draw up his own unilateral performance measurements for pitches. The results are fantastic.

'This is Hall Place Gardens where we have an open space of 65 hectares. There are two rugby pitches, seven football pitches and cricket pitches.' Mr Cannon is justifiably proud of this public facility. Right next to the A2 dual carriageway, it has football pitches that manage to look like bowling greens, even after a full season of two matches every weekend.

The new contracts for the maintenance of Hall Place do not stipulate how many times to mow the grass, they give a maximum and minimum length that the grass should be. They also give requirements for factors such as bounce, dryness and evenness. Initially the workers were puzzled. Where were the job tickets? But, says Mr Cannon, they soon warmed to the approach.

'With CCT, we felt that the industry was being de-skilled because everybody just relied on a piece of paper to work from. Now, having passed the responsibility back to the contractor, the sense of pride in the work and the skills are coming back. We just let them get on with it.'

Better value, then, for the council, higher quality pitches for players and, most importantly of all, less work for the casualty departments. Hall Place is a green and pleasant testimony to what Peter Dury would like to see implemented everywhere. 'The worst part of it is that most of the senior council officers aren't even aware of these tests, and many who are, don't understand them. If they did, sport would be much much safer.'

Bexley's enlightened policy remains the exception. Seventeen years after Peter was first ready to produce his standards, they remain unpublished by the Institute of Groundsmanship. Waiting for the Eurocrats, as the Sports Turf Research Institute is doing, seems unending. In the mean time the lawyers continue to make a killing and Mr Dury continues to earn from a sideline as an expert witness in claims cases.

When claims are settled, the bill is usually picked up by David Forster's company, Zurich Municipal, which insures four-out-of-five local authorities. David would welcome performance quality standards because in the long run they would stop most of the claims being made, and in the short run would simplify matters. 'The standards need to be achievable and acceptable to all parties,' he told me in the board room of Zurich's headquarters in Hampshire. 'There's no point in producing guidelines which are unachievable and unsustainable – no one will benefit from that. Also, who's to say what a pitch would be like from one day to the next? Any guidelines will have to be flexible enough to cope with the weather.'

After nearly 30 years of consultation – years when progress has been repeatedly held up by bureaucracy, politics and splits among the experts – it is reasonable to believe that all the parties involved are now happy with the standards that have so far been agreed. But, even when these guidelines are applied, there will obviously be a delay while the necessary improvements are made and before the benefits are fully appreciated by the players.

Two years after Paul Gibson sustained his injury, the dispute over whether or not the pitch was to blame has not been resolved. Until standards are accepted and implemented casualty departments can expect a steady trickle of footballers with similar complaints to Paul. 'You, in the soccer boots – the doctor can see you now.'

CHAPTER EIGHT

Pirates and Border Raiders
England's Outlawed Youth Soccer Leagues

It is hard to imagine a prouder man than Cledwyn Ashford as he walks down the main corridor of the Mold primary school where he is headmaster. Hanging on the corridor walls next to brightly colured paintings and displays are signed shirts, photographs, caps and other mementoes of the boys who have gone on from playing for the Deeside (now Flintshire) area representative team that he manages, to reach the top.

In glass cases are souvenirs of Deeside School's old boys and it reads like a 'Who's Who?' of recent Welsh football. Ian Rush, Kevin Ratcliffe, Gary Speed, Barry Horne and Tony Norman are all graduates of the Deeside academy, and are all honoured in the school corridor.

Mr Ashford, though, is most proud when he reaches a space on the wall reserved for the cream of his crop – the one who got away as far as Welsh football is concerned – England's newest superstar, Michael Owen.

The pleasure Cledwyn Ashford gets from his memories is tempered by the Welsh FA's decision that all boys of primary school age must play small-sided football. After producing a number of internationals through the traditional eleven-a-side system, Cledwyn Ashford was annoyed by the move to seven-a-side football. 'They did not think it through and it came out on a block: stop eleven-a-side as from this date. But we knew the situation we were in, knew the standards we had achieved, knew that these boys were playing to the best standard possible... '

The move, however, was vigorously defended by Jimmy Shoulder, Development Officer for the Football Association of Wales. 'We're interested in giving children the opportunity to develop their strengths, co-ordination, athleticism and technical abilities. To do that, you have to scale the whole thing down. You cannot have them taking part in something designed for full-sized adults.'

Barry Horne went on from Deeside to play 59 times for Wales, and, also in a long career, played for Southampton, Everton and Huddersfield Town. He remembers well the football education he received in North Wales.

'In my primary school year we played 33 games and won 33. We won the three main cup tournaments that were available at the time, so we were known as a very successful team. When you consider some of the teams we were playing against and consider the fact that our team was from a relatively small area, it is remarkable really.'

Apart from producing international footballers such as Barry Horne, Cledwyn Ashford is proud of the fact that when the boys went away to tournaments, such as the Jersey Festival, they learnt about more than just being able to play football: 'We used to teach them how to behave – they had to behave or they were out of the side. We used to stay in hotels; they were part of a small group of boys who had to get on with each other. I believe they became better boys because of all this. Headmasters noticed and commented on that.' But, due to being forced into small-sided football, he now fears that such away-trips will be thing of the past.

For some, the weekly game of full-sided football is only possible after a tense week of clandestine phone calls and agreements on secret rendezvous' just so their ten-year-old off-spring can take the field.

The reason for this cloak-and-dagger operation is that, like its Welsh counterpart, the English FA has forced boys under ten to play small-sided football, with small goals, small pitches and different rules, instead of the eleven-a-side football played by their heroes.

The plans are part of the 'Charter For Quality', written by Howard Wilkinson, the Football Association's Technical Director. Its aim is to ensure that the country's future footballers are not the traditional English worthy losers, but the next century's skilful heroic winners.

The central figure in the recommendations for the "Charter for Quality" is the player and his or her best interests. Attempting to provide quality experience for all young players at all levels is the over-riding principle.
(Football Association Charter for Quality, 1997)

Wilkinson's aims are to take young footballers off full-size pitches with full-sized goals, to stop them chasing a ball around and trying to boot it the length of the field, and to place more emphasis on skill and passing with more opportunity to see more of the action.

But there are many parents who do not want their children to play in the new small-sided leagues and who are prepared to risk a lifetime's ban from the game if they are caught. They help to organize – and take their children to – unaffiliated or 'Pirate' leagues outside the umbrella of the Football Association and their local county bodies. One such league in south London is run by Ken, along with Terry – not their real names – who, like so many of the people who are involved in the leagues, wish to remain anonymous.

'We've got 50 or so clubs in our League playing unaffiliated football, and I would not like to expose any of them to county officials or whatever, who might take action against them.'

These South London pirates have every right to be fearful: Dave Bettridge, manager of Tonbridge and Sevenoaks Under-9s was banned for life by the Kent FA for fielding eleven players in his team. His club was also fined £1000. Mr Bettridge claims that he and his club were made scapegoats. He says there were around 30 other teams playing in the League at eleven-a-side which the Kent FA were aware of, making the decision even harsher. After an appeal, Mr Bettridge's ban was reduced and he was able to apply to Lancaster Gate to manage again in December 1999.

By then, small-sided football for nine-year-olds will be in

full swing, but Dave Bettridge is sure that teams of nine-year olds will continue to play eleven-a-side unaffiliated football and that this type of football will flourish. This, according to Ken, is already the case in south London. 'I think we are the mainstream. I think if you asked the FA – it hasn't come to us and asked our opinion – I think we are the mainstream. There are more eleven-a-side games going on than seven-a-side games, and I think the FA is going to have to do something quite big to change our minds.'

For Howard Wilkinson however, charged with the responsibility of finding the formula for success, the small-sided game which, along with the plans for soccer academies, forms the bulk of the 'Charter for Quality' is the only way forward if England is to develop the world's best players. The former Leeds United and Sheffield Wednesday boss says he is convinced we will be left behind unless we embrace it quickly.

'They're now playing small-sided soccer in the streets of Africa and South America and all the poorer parts of the world. It's not small-sided in the sense that it's lines and goals, but small-sided in the sense that kids come together and play. Girls can play, boys can play – its fairer on everybody. You don't necessarily find yourself stuck in goal. And because it doesn't have the connotations that eleven-a-side has in terms of strategy and tactics and management, it leads to a much better atmosphere around the pitch. Parents or the manager find it difficult to associate with, say, Alex Ferguson in a game where there is no need for tactics or strategy, there's just need for some-one to make sure that the kids behave themselves well and that the games are refereed well.'

When the idea of small-sided football was first raised in 1995, 500 young footballers and their parents descended in noisy protest on the Football Association's headquarters at Lancaster Gate. As for the 'pirates' who defy the FA and continue with the traditional full-sided game, Wilkinson feels they are misguided and doing their kids more harm than good. 'Because it's there, it doesn't make it right. Eventually the whole country will be playing small-sided football up to the appropriate age. It's

fairer on children. I watch games on a Sunday morning in which
my boys play, the goals are far too big and the pitch is too long.
If a factory inspector was brought round, he'd take them to court
on grounds of cruelty to children .'

Howard Wilkinson's passionate, if somewhat exaggerated
argument will not sway the south London 'pirates'. Although
their pleas to the Football Association to have their League affiliated have fallen on deaf ears, they are convinced that their
method of football has its place. 'We have said that we'll provide
football for kids who want to play in that particular football
environment. It's a controlled environment and run well. All the
kids are registered and all will play in the right age groups.
There's registration cards and everything else necessary to
accompany managers to a game. It's all controlled by rules.'

Such is their desire for their children to play in the full-
sided game they will go to extraordinary lengths to avoid being
detected. According to Bob, when a team joins no questions are
asked and no names are given. 'There could be some clubs which
change their name – I don't ask for history, just ask for a piece of
paper which we can identify them by. Generally we know who
we are going to play at the beginning of every year, but we don't
know where until a couple of days before the game.'

Parents, such as Ken, know that as from the 1999-2000
season when small-side football for the Under-10s is brought in,
they will be forced totally underground. 'We'll have to change
our name because the name we have is the name of the town
we're in! We won't be able have a home ground, we'll have to
play our matches at the last minute at lots of various grounds.
We'll have to play in open parks with unofficial goals set up or
use mobile goals. I think it'll be even more cloak and dagger
than the game we have now.'

Bob and Ken are family men who hold responsible jobs
with large multi-national companies in the centre of London.
They admit the situation they find themselves in every weekend
is ridiculous, but, according to Ken, the plans drawn up by the FA
just do not make sense. 'I'm not opposed to small-sided football.
If the product is good, if the people see it has certain benefits

they will participate. But there are a lot of problems with small-sided football, especially in the winter.'

The idea is that teams will play several matches a day – not ideal for parents and shivering nine-year-olds. 'Standing around in the cold and wet waiting for games will, I think, create a demand for unaffiliated eleven-a-side football and I don't think the FA will be able to stop that.'

Back in North Wales, Cledwyn Ashford says he and his Deeside colleagues attempted to consult with the Welsh FA, but it stood its ground. 'We begged and begged, and carried on for a season. The following year we also carried on, and it was then the that FAW became quite bombastic, saying: "You can't carry on. We will not allow you to". And that is where we came unstuck. They were saying that no side in Wales could play eleven-a-side at Under-11s, so we had no opposition. We decided to play the English teams, but were told that they would be reported to the English Schools' Football Association and would be told not to play Welsh teams at eleven-a-side. We contacted the English Association and it said: "We'd love to play, but we can't. We've been told not to play you"'.

Cledwyn Ashford and his co-manager, Dave Nicholas, feel they were bullied by the FAW and told in no uncertain terms that they had no choice other than to play seven-a-side football. 'We were more or less told if you don't stop now then all sorts of things could happen. The insinuation was that the boys who played at this level would not go any higher than that, and that myself and Mr Nicholas would not be able to take a team. We were part of the Welsh schoolboys and wouldn't be covered to run teams because nobody would insure us. So, we were really under threat and tried to act in a professional manner.'

As the architect of the move to small-sided football in Wales, Jimmy Shoulder is understandably defensive about his ideas, and claims that there are already good results. 'There's no question now that through our Centres of Excellence pro-gramme in Wales – the best couple of dozen youngsters from the Under-12s, Under-14s and Under-15s – it's manifest which children played mini-football before the age of twelve. They are better technically than other children, and are much more confident as well.'

Drive the short distance up the A541 from Mold to Wrexham and there is evidence of yet more resentment to small-sided football. Brian Johnson, who runs the Wrexham and District Youth Football League, claims that he received too short a notice when the time came for his teams to change to small sides, and that this caused many problems, most of them financial.

Mr Johnson attended meetings with FAW officials where, having raised his concerns, he was told that small-sided football was compulsory. He, too, felt he was being threatened. 'We received correspondence from the FAW which virtually said, by insinuation rather than words, that we would be suspended or banned. But when we had conversations with various FA officials, we were told outright exactly what was meant: that the league officials down to the players would officially be suspended from all means of association football.'

Such is the nature of the small-sided game that new equipment – including new costly smaller goal posts – is needed. Mr Johnson, like Cledwyn Ashford, approached the FAW to ask for more time. He was told that he had to comply or face the consequences. It was a simple choice – play football at eleven-a-side or face being banned from playing altogether.

Jimmy Shoulder admits that there was a mixed reception to the plans to bring in seven-a-side football for Under-11s, and that he was not entirely surprised. 'No matter what you introduce, people will resist change. The sort of people who resisted me were ordinary mums and dads who were running sides for youngsters in their own time. But their lack of expertise led them to mimic the adult game.'

Although Mr Johnson is now a convert to the small-sided game, he still feels bitter about the way it was introduced by the FAW. As in south London, the opposition to the new game has led some parents in North Wales to take drastic action.

Tom Hughes runs a junior side in the Chester area just over the border from Brian Johnson's league. Since the football authorities in Wales introduced the idea of seven-a-side football he has known a number of teams and individuals that have made secret cross-border raids to play English teams at eleven-a-side. He says that he has played – and will continue to play – teams that want to participate in full-sided matches.

'I am very aware that there is strong resentment especially in the Clwyd League in North Wales and in one or two clubs in the Wrexham area as well. They come across to play pre-season friendlies, and even during the season when they have free weeks. And what they do is change their name to an English club which is not affiliated to the Cheshire FA and play under that name for the friendly which is eleven-a-side football.'

The momentum for disregarding the wishes of both the FA in England and Wales is growing according to Tom Hughes, who says that his club, Newton Juniors, will continue to play full-sided football. 'We have a very strong view within Newton about the way we would like to go, and we will take on board all the other clubs of which there are 18 spread from Liverpool through to West Kirby to the countryside of Cheshire. And we will counsel those people to see how they want to approach that situation, and will give a lead as to how Newton thinks it should go. They have no reason to doubt our word as they have been with us for the past four or five seasons in terms of the fixture programme. Our view is that there will be a continuation of non-affiliated eleven-a-side football.'

Pressure from Lancaster Gate will not deter Tom Hughes or other mangers. He has spoken to a number inside and outside his area who would not go on the record for fear of being tracked down by the FAW and banned from the game. 'They don't want to put their clubs in jeopardy. They fear there will be retribution from the Welsh FA with regard to them coming across and playing friendlies at eleven-a-side at Under-10s and Under-9s level.'

Just as schoolboy footballers are crossing the border to surreptitiously take on teams in England, so, according to Tom Hughes, so the notion of defying the authorities to carry on playing eleven-a-side football is a very real one.

'I know of five or six clubs at this present moment who have said they will participate. I am not going to name them but they feel absolutely as we do. I am speaking purely from a league in the Chester area, I assure you, though there will be rogue leagues in the Liverpool area.'

Brian Johnson knows of players from his league in Wrexham who had to go to England so they could play full-sided football.

'We were aware that it was happening, but all we could do was inform parents what the implications were and leave the decision up to them. If the FAW was aware of this, then we didn't hear of any action.'

A request to Jimmy Shoulder for the introduction of the new game to be staggered so that leagues and their clubs could prepare properly, was refused with an added warning, according to Brian Johnson, if they didn't comply. 'It would have meant that we would have totally lost all of our affiliation through our local football association through to Welsh FA. We would have been totally banned, suspended from organized football in Wales.'

Brian Johnson's choice had been made for him. If a ten-year-old footballer from North Wales wanted to play football in England, says Mr Johnson, he would not be able to unless he had permission from none other than world football's governing body.

'There is such a thing as international clearance for players right down to junior footballers. They need this to play in England. If they don't have this, the FAW could get in touch with the English FA and have them suspended until it is sorted out. That's something I am not very happy about, but FIFA's rule is that all players need clearance to move from one country to play in another.'

The attitude to the small-sided game by its detractors has angered Jimmy Shoulder. 'They're very misguided people. They're doing it for their own ends, not for the children. They do not understand that it is better for the children to play small-sided football. They want to be seen as the manager of the championship team, as the coach of the winning or best team and don't really understand that we're organizing the game for the benefit of the children, not for our own benefit.'

From a shed at the top of his garden in Kent, ex-Policeman

Alan Clarke runs the London Youth Football Association. He also runs the Tandridge Junior League in south London, the second biggest in the country, and sits on an FA working party looking into the future of youth football in England. Despite his position within the FA he admits that there is more opposition to the introduction of small-sided football than the authorities realize and that the 'pirate leagues' will grow. 'All it will do is push people further underground. They will hide deeper from us. The only way you can deal with this is to persuade people that small football is best for boys of this age.'

That is not going to be an easy task for the FA. According to the 'pirate' football parents, the leagues they run are well organized, well attended, successful and do not need the Football Association. In the case of the Tandridge League in South London, run by Mr Clarke, the objections are not so much idealistic as logistic.

'We have 52 teams playing eleven-a-side football at Under-10 level this year, which, in theory, means we'd have 104 teams wanting to play small-sided football next year. Now the capacity I have at the present time amongst my member clubs, to provide small-sided football for Under-9s, Under-8s and Under-7s, is just about being reached by them providing their own pitches, hiring from schools and buying the soccer goals. To provide a game for double that number of Under-10s boys in my League – probably about 750 boys next season – is something I don't think we can achieve without a great deal of help from the Football Association.'

Money has been promised to help pay for the new equipment that small-sided football requires and every county has been asked to prepare a budget to implement the new game. But the amounts the FA is talking about are, according to Mr Clarke, not enough to ensure that every child who wants to play football is able to do so.

Mr Clarke is also concerned about the space that the new game will need. This, he concedes, will not be a problem for county associations, but will lead to problems for inner-city areas such as London.

'I have had words with colleagues in the shire counties and they don't seem to have a problem providing facilities. But in inner London there's a huge shortage of recreational space. There is a reduction in football pitches for senior players which is of great concern to my senior body, the London Football Association, and I don't know where we are going to find facilities to take on thousands of boys into small-sided football in central London.'

The debate over junior football rages on. Jimmy Shoulder is confident that those who doubt its merits will soon see that the days of small boys chasing a ball around a pitch built for adults are best forgotten. 'I won't say they don't know what they are talking about. What I am saying is that all of the evidence – and I speak with over 20 years' experience as an international coach – points to the fact that the best way to produce sport for children is to have modified rules and modified games. Whether that results in somebody becoming an international player or someone becoming an excellent player for the Black Bull on a Sunday morning, you'll maximize their potential and enjoyment.'

Howard Wilkinson and Jimmy Shoulder are at one in their desire to see small-sided football played at schoolboy level, and view it as the best way to produce good footballers who also enjoy the game. And that, according to Jimmy Shoulder, is the key point. 'If you play in a football match where you have 50 touches instead of 25, you will improve more. That's just common sense.'

Despite having to keep one step ahead of the FA, players in the south London 'pirates league', – according to Bob and Ken their kids enjoy their eleven-a-side football unaware that they are breaking any rules. 'We've tried to keep them away from our feelings. We want them to enjoy themselves. We don't want them to feel under any sort of pressure, and I think what we're doing is something for fun rather than being too serious at this stage. We enjoy ourselves on Saturdays and Sundays and so do the boys, and that's the way we have to keep it. I don't want the boys to be under any sort of pressure.'

The football authorities of both England and Wales are committed to the implementation of small-sided football. For Howard Wilkinson in particular, who has travelled the world in order to find the best coaching methods for a country that repeatedly fails to deliver on the international scene, there is tremendous responsibility.

The battle for the hearts and minds of junior football is going to be long and hard with more rumours of pirate or unaffiliated leagues springing up in other parts of the country in defiance of the FA. Meanwhile, along the border between England and Wales, junior teams – using assumed names in defiance of not just the Welsh football authorities, but the world-governing body – will cross over to take on teams at eleven-a-side.

The battle will no doubt continue in a world of false names, secrecy, threats of bans and clandestine meetings – all in the name of Under-10s' football.

CHAPTER NINE

Just Child's Play?
How the Big Clubs are Targeting Your Kids

Howard Wilkinson has a dream. The Football Association's technical director wants to make England's young footballers the best in the world. But are his plans turning the playground into a battle ground; and could children be the losers?

A typical scene: school has finished and hundreds of kids around the UK are dashing home to get changed. After a hurried tea, they sling their football kit into the car boot and jump into the passenger seat beside their mum or dad. It is a routine they have come to know well. While their friends are playing computer games or sitting in front of the box, they are off to spend the evening training at a professional football club. They are the young soccer élite – Academy Lads.

One of them is Richard Carrington, a fresh-faced, leggy mid-fielder from Dronfield Woodhouse in Sheffield. At 15, in his GCSE year at school, Richard was given permission to take Monday after-noons off to train at Barnsley Football Club. The programme is run by an ex-headmaster and includes a mix of outdoor work and indoor training in a small gym under one of the stands.

'I come on Mondays, Wednesdays and Fridays for training. Mondays out of school and Wednesday and Friday night,' he says. 'It's about six or seven hours in all. It's hard work, but it's good because you get good stuff out of it. We do a lot of ball work, passing and control to get good touch.'

The first club to show an interest in Richard was Rotherham United, when he was just 11. He also spent time at Blackburn's academy. His dad Michael is convinced of the benefits. 'The whole idea of football coaching is altering now,' he says. 'You need to get the skill levels at eight, nine years old, and these academies offer that. What you can't learn is the physical side – that comes naturally. It's the skills that you learn and if you don't go to an academy you are not going to get them, so you are at a disadvantage for later on.'

It was a re-write of Football Association rules in 1993 that changed the way clubs could nurture talent. The academies followed: training centres attached to individual clubs, where youngsters could learn the techniques and intricacies of the game with the best facilities available. The aim was to usher in a new generation of technically-adept English players with the skills to match their foreign counterparts. The final step came with the closure of the National School of Excellence at Lilleshall, which had previously taken the cream of the crop.

Howard Wilkinson was a driving force behind the change. His CV includes two years teaching at a grammar school as well as managing three teams to promotion, Leeds to a League title, and a very brief stint as England caretaker. He is by repute strong-willed, even bloody-minded, but also knowledgeable and deep-thinking. He makes no bones about his priorities, 'I'm looking for England to produce players capable of winning the World Cup and of playing for their club teams and dominating Europe in the European club competitions.

'We had a very successful experiment at Lilleshall with selected boys over ten years. We decided that we could now, with justification, extend its benefits. Instead of having 15 to 17 boys benefiting, we decided that as many boys as possible should benefit but for that to happen the clubs would have to operate very similar operations to Lilleshall.'

Wilkinson mapped the way forward in a half-inch-thick document called *A Charter For Quality*. Among other things, it aims to encourage boys and girls to play football and to let the most talented children get coaching at top clubs. Academies can take children from the age of eight, for up to three hours a week, with the hours rising as they get older. Homework and study areas are provided, each academy must have a full-time education officer, and the *Charter* insists school work and welfare must not suffer.

Every Premier League club and at least 14 Nationwide League clubs are licensed to run academies. Many have superb facilities; Liverpool's cost around £10 million. Players under 11 will only be allowed to play seven-a-side games and no boy can play more than 30 games a year. All players must live within a maximum travelling distance (one hour each way for eight to 13-year-olds, and 90 minutes for older boys).

Former Crystal Palace manager Alan Smith is now the director of Fulham's academy at Motspur Park, in a leafy Surrey suburb. He has an unrivalled reputation for caring for young players. He told the *Guardian*, 'Our European colleagues have been laughing at us for our island mentality over the past 20 years and results at youth level show how far behind we are. Now we can start catching up and produce a whole new generation of well-equipped, technically gifted players.'

It seemed as though the English game was finally getting its act together over youth development and meeting all those complaints about players who couldn't pass or trap a ball without falling over. But as copies of the *Charter for Quality* began to land on doormats around the country, it soon became clear that some people were unhappy – very unhappy – about many of its elements.

One of the first bodies to voice objections was the National Council for School Sport (NCSS), an umbrella organization representing 31 sports. 'I'm afraid we weren't consulted by the FA at all,' says its executive officer, Pat Smith. 'The English Schools FA got in touch with us and we had several meetings with them and with some of the teacher unions because we were concerned about some of the suggestions that the FA were making.'

Pat Smith sees good things in the *Charter* and does not dispute that it may produce excellent players. His concern is, at what cost? He has heard a catalogue of complaints from his members and in a statement the NCSS listed the following five main concerns:

• The emphasis on a single sport for many children

- The age at which this specialization will start
- Encouraging pupils not to represent their school and area football teams
- The commitment of time expected from children
- The expectations of the children and their parents

Others chipped in. Youth teams around the country claimed they were being decimated by scouts picking off their best boys; schools complained about a lack of communication and teachers pointed out that professional football clubs were hardly the best people to look after children's welfare.

'What we then did was to contact other sports who might be affected, others with a professional basis like rugby league, rugby union, cricket, tennis, athletics, and we had a meeting of the schools associations of those,' says Mr Smith. 'Everybody without doubt was worried about some aspects of this charter.'

Defenders of the academy system were quick to hit back. Kit Carson at Peterborough United said, 'The academies were set up for highly talented people. Is it best for a child's footballing development that he should be playing for St Blobsworth secondary Under-12s when he could be playing a team from Ajax? Some heads think their school's image is lessened if they don't win local cups.'

And Alan Smith at Fulham said, 'Coaches have to declare they have no convictions for molesting children, and must have proper qualifications and understand diet and nutrition. And one of the full-time staff must be an education and welfare officer. We liaise with the schools on education and homework as well as encouraging them to let the boys play their actual matches for us in a league of other academy teams.'

Howard Wilkinson foresaw the possibility that not everyone would be thrilled with his ideas. One section of the *Charter* is headlined 'Avoidance of Conflict'. Unfortunately the crucial area of liaison between club and school – the most likely source of friction – appears to have been left mainly to the individuals concerned in each area. It soon became apparent that many schools were unhappy at the behaviour of club representatives. And, as the implications of the *Charter* sank in, some of the criticisms started to go far deeper.

So who is right? What is best for a young, active child showing sporting potential at an early age and what should parents do if their son is asked to attend an academy? *On The Line* canvassed some of the people the FA had failed to consult and asked them about the key areas of concern.

• The emphasis on a single sport for many children

Critics are worried that the amount of time children spend concentrating on football will prevent them from doing other beneficial activities.

Peter Warburton is an expert in the physical education of children. As director of sport at Durham University, he teaches the teachers of tomorrow. He is unequivocal about the drawbacks of children concentrating on one sport from an early age.

'This is a massive area of concern. I would definitely say the balance of the programme we have now, which is games, gymnastics, dance, outdoor pursuits, swimming and athletics is the ideal for any child. We really need to be giving them a clear balance throughout their time in school from four to eleven with opportunities in all those areas. I have a concern we're not going to get that. I'm not a great believer in saying children can't cope with a lot of physical activity. My concern is, it isn't going to be that balanced. Their whole life is going to be soccer.'

Others share his view. John Robson is chairman of the English Schools FA and a senior teacher, also in Durham. 'I believe that between the ages of nine and fourteen boys and girls should have the widest possible experience they can, not just in sport but in music, drama and other fields. All of that will be affected if boys go four times a week to an academy. I think certain clubs are worse than others. They want the best boys and their whole *raison d'etre* is to get the best boys for their club.'

He believes that once different sports realize that football is creaming off the best talent, they will try to do the same, provoking a tug-of-war with children in the middle. 'I fear that will be the case because they can't afford not to. They want the excellent boys. The only problem is, the excellent boys at rugby, swimming, basketball,whatever, are the same boys who are excellent at football.'

In fact, it is already happening. Now that football has thrown its hat into the playground, others are doing the same, as Ron Tennick, technical administrator for school and youth for the Rugby Football Union, ruefully admits. 'One or two rugby clubs are starting academies, anxious to pick up kids and teach them to play rather than have them taught at school. There is some concern with the RFU that this may not be the best way forward. The best people to teach are those who have been taught to teach and not coaches who may not understand that much about children and child development. I think the whole thing's crazy.

'Everyone's doing the same thing. Every game now has a mini version to make it easy for children to play in order to grab their interest. But experience also shows that the interest span for the average player in any sport or hobby is four to six years. We're finding a huge fall-out when children leave school because they've had enough and want to do something else.

'These children should be allowed the option to play as many sports as possible from eight to 14, then start to think about specializing, but taking into the sport they choose all the skills they have learned from all the other sports, whether it be dance or rugby or cricket or whatever. There's always something one sport can learn from another.'

Mr Tennick's opposite number at the Rugby Football League is associate director for development Tom O'Donovan. His sport has to face the reality that its 'M62 corridor' hinterland is a soccer hotbed with the likes of Liverpool and Everton at one end, Leeds, the Sheffield clubs and numerous others at the other, and Manchester United, Manchester City, Blackburn Rovers and Bolton Wanderers in the middle. In a battle for talent, rugby league is almost always going to come off second best, although Mr O'Donovan believes early specialization in one game would leave everyone the loser.

'It certainly would. It would even hit soccer in the end. At that young age group I'm sure there's a Beckham and a Fowler there and there will be future rugby union and rugby league internationals of the like of Shaun Edwards. But youngsters at that age aren't dedicated soccer or rugby league players and need the opportunity to play other sports. A young soccer player at eight or nine may well become a superb talent at rugby or basketball and shouldn't be pigeon-holed that early.'

The appendix at the back of the *Charter for Quality* contains a list of those who were consulted before it was written. The list makes no mention of the governing bodies of any other sport. Howard Wilkinson says he did look at other sports, but his focus was in learning from their training methods. 'In my job as a football manager I looked at other sports all the time to see if there were things they were doing which could be of benefit to us and help us win football matches,' he said.

• The age at which this specialization will start

One of the most controversial aspects of the *Charter* is the starting age of eight for professional tuition; the document actually says 'under nine' which could theoretically include toddlers, although the clubs seem so far to have stuck to eight as a minimum.

Neil Webb was a product of the old system, where children played five or six games a week on big pitches with few qualified coaches. The emphasis was on quantity not quality. He came through it to play for England, Manchester United and Nottingham Forest. Now his two sons, Luke and Joshua, are following in his footsteps. He believes they will benefit from a far superior system.

Luke was asked to sign for Arsenal in 1998, at the age of 12. 'We thought long and hard, had a look round and went up and had talk with them. The set-up was magnificent. They look after kids and I was impressed. There was nothing like it when I was a kid. We felt that at 12 years of age the time was right for Luke to progress. He had outgrown his school friends in playing football, and if he wanted to have the chance of becoming a footballer he needed to progress and what better way?'

Significantly, though, Neil wouldn't let his eight-year-old, Joshua, join an academy. 'He plays Sunday seven-a-side football which is good for him, 15 minutes each way. He loves that. Crystal Palace asked if he could go along for trials for their Under-nines. Three other lads from his team went along and they all got in, which is great. I decided eight was too young. If he went along at eight and they said, "No", I felt that would be too devastating for him. He's enjoying his football, plays for school on Wednesdays and I think that's enough. I told them to come back when he was ten and still developing. I just didn't want to take his innocence away. I wanted him to love football.'

Pat Smith rues the trend. 'Unfortunately there is such a competition now for talented youngsters that the clubs want to get them at as early an age as possible. Now that's very sad because it doesn't give the youngster a youth and I feel that if they start coaching or putting pressure on youngsters at too early an age the youngster may well drop out of the game. They'll be saturated with it.'

Ron Tennick of the RFU has even stronger views. He thinks eight is 'ridiculously' young to start training at pro clubs. 'All sports have fallen into the same trap. They believe that if they don't target children that early they may never get them into their sport. But they're targeting them too early, they're starting to play at six, seven, eight and then by 18, after ten years in the sport, they've had enough and when they leave school, they look for something else to do. They are going to finish up with people who can play, but they ain't going to have a great deal of intelligence to do anything else. That's why I think it's mad to start so young.'

Incredibly, some clubs are spotting and logging children as young as four. And pressure is already mounting. One club community officer said, 'A lot of clubs are frightened that if they miss someone at age eight or nine, someone else will snap them up.'

Yet somehow the message has failed to filter through. 'I have not heard any criticisms from other sports,' says Howard Wilkinson. 'As far as I'm concerned there are plenty of examples of sports which start earlier than eight and I have seen no evidence that starting at that age, provided the appropriate care is given, is in any way harmful to them.

'At what age should they start training at clubs? At what age should children start going to school? It's not a question of too young or too old. It's a question of what sort of care are they given, what are they capable of accepting, what sort of experience are they being involved in, are they doing it voluntarily, is it harming them and most importantly, are they enjoying it?'

• Encouraging pupils not to represent school and area teams

On this point, Howard Wilkinson is adamant. 'The academies aren't going to discourage children from playing for their schools or other sports. The playing experiences of a child will be enhanced because the child can only play a maximum number of games. The rule quite clearly states that the choice of which team a child plays for will be that of the parents – in conjunction with the club and the school – but it will be that of the parents and the child.'

Unfortunately, it appears that many of the professional clubs have not been listening. Pat Smith of the National Council for School Sport has come across numerous examples of academy lads being discouraged from playing for their school, county or youth side.

'There *is* pressure put on children not to play for their school,' he says. 'Now that's a shame because part of going to school is owing a loyalty to the school. If they're attracted away from that, I think that undermines that loyalty.'

In October 1998, five Midlands county schools football associations banned professional club scouts from all matches. The associations – covering Staffordshire, West Midlands, Warwickshire, Herefordshire and Shropshire – were concerned at the behaviour of some of the clubs. John Dunford, general secretary of the Secondary Heads Association, said, 'We feel football clubs are being unreasonable. They are not taking into account the needs of the schools or the development of young people.'

Malcolm Berry, chief executive of the English Schools FA, said, 'The selfishness of some clubs searching for the so-called élite youngster is removing the spirit from the schoolboy game and verges on exploitation.'

It is not just school and county teams that are affected. One Premier League academy even stopped one of its players from turning out for the England youth team. And local youth sides, for so long the breeding ground for talent, are facing a tough struggle to hang on to their players.

On a muddy, floodlit pitch on the north-east coast of England, Graham Hunt coaches South Tyneside Under-14s. They're a good local youth team, one of thousands around the country. Mr Hunt's experience with his Under-13 side, however, has soured him on the idea of academies.

'Our Under-13s managed to start the season but with the academies starting up they came in and just took the whole team. So we lost a complete team this year. They left the team with seven kids. We just couldn't build a team that quick to get it out for the following Sunday so we had to forfeit. Every one of those kids were contracted. We are contracting kids all the time but it seems that to the academies they are not worth the paper they're written on.'

He says all of the north-east youth sides – including the famous Wallsend Boys which produced Alan Shearer and Paul Gascoigne – are suffering and scouts are no longer welcome.

'It's annoying now when they come. They could wipe your team out and it does bug you. Before you used to have a good relationship with scouts, but now it's getting to where you ain't going to want them at your games. As soon as the scout walks in and waves a contract under their nose, they're gone. You can see the stars in their eyes.'

• The commitment of time expected from children

The *Charter* recognizes that it is undesirable for children to have to travel long distances after school and at weekends in order to train. It therefore limits journey times to an hour each way for the very young, rising to an hour and a half for older children. But no-one is policing this and even if they were, critics say it still takes a big chunk out of a youngster's life. It could mean twelve hours a week in a car for a child in his exam year.

'There's no time for the youngster to play other sports or even go to discos,' says Pat Smith of the NCSS. 'And when are they supposed to do their homework? I know clubs say, "Oh, yes, we provide a place for them to do homework and a tutor", but if a child has travelled for an hour, done an hour-and-a-half's training, and has an hour's travel home again, they're not going to be keen to do their homework at that time, are they?'

In any case, it appears that the journey rules are not always obeyed. Richard Carrington, now at the Barnsley FC academy, previously trained at a club much further away from his home.'My mum would pick me up straight after school, I'd go home and have a little bit to eat, then set off. I'd have a bit of a rest when I got there, then I did my training and came back. Some nights I was getting back at midnight and I was a bit tired in the morning.'

The constant quest for talent means that clubs will cast their nets as far as they can. Ron Tennick points out that, on a good day, it would be possible to travel from, for example, Birmingham to Manchester in around 90 minutes, the set limit. 'All they are doing is sitting in the car, having a couple of hours soccer, sitting in a car, going to school the next day, and then doing the same thing the next night. When do they fit in other interests, hobbies, homework? We are going to finish up with some people who can play but who ain't got a great deal of intelligence to do anything else because they spend so much time sitting in cars going up and down motorways. Which seems absolutely ludicrous.'

Clubs are also prepared to go to ingenious lengths to meet the restrictions and ring-fence young talent. In January 1999 it was reported that Derby County had become the first club to buy boarding places for its star apprentices at Repton, a leading independent school, which also happens to be well within the *Charter's* travel limits.

Clubs have even been known to encourage children to bunk off school to go training. In 1998, the English Schools FA fired off an angry letter to the Premier League about this.

'I know of one club which asked for a boy to be released on a Friday, every Friday, to be trialled for six to eight weeks,' says ESFA chairman Mr Robson. 'He was in year 11, his exam year. The head teacher refused, and refuses to discuss the matter further. We had a boy at my own school who went three mornings a week for physiotherapy in year ten; again, in the first year of an exam course.

'One of our greatest problems is communications between the schools and football clubs, partly because clubs were allowed to start their academies without having the full staffing. Many have only just appointed education and welfare officers who are crucial in links with the school.

'We have to respect the *Charter* because we are members of the FA – and we do respect the *Charter* – we just have certain educational concerns. We are constantly being written to and telephoned by head teachers and PE staff about instances where clubs are not carrying out best practice.'

• The expectations of the children and their parents

The 'soccer dad' is fast becoming the English equivalent of the American 'tennis mom' – pushy, overly competitive and obsessively ambitious for their offspring. The huge wealth now washing through the game has become an added incentive for parents who dream of their child making the big time. But the failure rate in football is enormous.

Having played the game at the highest level, Neil Webb knows the pitfalls. He feels it is easy for parents to be seduced by the glitz of the game. 'I think certain parents will be blinded by the glamour of going into an academy, especially with the financial rewards in game. They'll be blinkered into pushing their son into being a top-class footballer.'

This finds echoes elsewhere. 'Perhaps in the glamour of being wooed by a pro-soccer club, particularly in the Premier League,' says Tom O'Donovan of the RFL, 'people may miss the point that the chances of making the grade may be very slim. We should ensure that parents are made aware of the possibility of failure.'

'How many of them are going to make it?' asks Peter Warburton of Durham University. 'And if they don't make it, what are they going to do? Without any question, building an academy structure around Premier League and other top sides around the country is going to mean that those sides are interested in one thing: in producing a football team that's going to get as far as it can possibly go. It has to have implications for the people they're working with.'

'I fear that with stars in their parents' eyes and their own eyes, they're going to be distracted from school work and think they've made it,' says Pat Smith of the NCSS. 'They've got to keep a balance.'

Howard Wilkinson remains strident. 'You will not stop children dreaming and aspiring to become a professional footballer, pulling on an England shirt, walking out at Wembley behind Alan Shearer, scoring the winning goal in a cup final. What academies are striving to do is to make sure those kids are given a better chance of succeeding while, at the same time, getting a rounded education and understanding the odds against them. All industries and professions have a failure rate. Not everyone who wants to be a doctor becomes one. Failure is part of our lives and it's up to football to help children deal with it. That's something we've not done very well in the past, but we are doing much better now and I think we'll get even better at it.'

It is still early days for the academies, and teething troubles are only to be expected. Much of the *Charter for Quality* is admirable and no one is suggesting that Howard Wilkinson and his FA colleagues don't care about children.

The clubs are another matter. Their record in encouraging values, sportsmanship and rounded development is hardly glowing. The winner-takes-all mentality of many managers and chairmen has led critics to suggest that Dracula is now in charge of the blood bank. If any other big business sought to train eight-year-olds for three hours a week after school, with a one-in-a-thousand chance of making them future employees, there would be an outcry. Add to that stories of six-year-old boys training at Premier League clubs, illegal payments to the parents of children and 13-year-olds being flown from South America for trials, and there is clear cause for concern.

Then there's the case of 15-year-old Jermaine Pennant. At the time of going to press, two football agents were facing FA charges over their handling of his £2 million transfer from Notts County to Arsenal. The charges relate to alleged inducements paid to Pennant's father.

Other countries, now a regular recruiting ground for British agents, are alarmed. 'The trade in children has got to stop,' pleaded French Sports Minister Marie-George Buffer in February 1999. 'Young talented players are treated like commodities. The trade raises serious questions about sporting ethics. We must legislate without delay.'

The British Government, however, adopted a rather different stance. In April 1999, in an extraordinary intervention, it announced it was earmarking £1 million to help set up academies at every Scottish Premier League club, with the possibility of a further £9 million being made available from the National Lottery and other sources provided the clubs could match the money pound-for-pound.

Tony Higgins, secretary of the Scottish players' union, said, 'This is a bold initiative that the Labour Party is proposing and it will provide a solution to the problems of youth development. The way forward for Scottish football is for players to be reared from an early age.'

In that word 'reared' there is a disturbing undertone. And quite what the Government is doing giving taxpayers' money to a business that patently doesn't need it, is a question some Scottish newspaper columnists have been asking.

At almost at the same time as the announcement, Celtic released 11 young players who had failed to establish themselves in the first team. With the huge increase in foreign players coming to the UK, the opportunities for home-grown talent are growing smaller, and more and more youngsters are going to end up on the scrapheap, rejected at such an early age.

'Gone are the days when people like Denis Compton could play football *and* cricket for England,' says Pat Smith. 'Things have now reached such a high standard that you must specialize. But there must be a balance between a child's education, his youth and the specialization which is necessary to reach a high standard.'

CHAPTER TEN

Soccer Slaves

The Young Players Dumped on the Streets by Ruthless Agents

Living in an abandoned bus, cold and hungry, wasn't exactly what Timi had in mind when he was promised a glittering career in European football.

An engaging and articulate young man, he showed talent from the time he first kicked a ball as a seven-year-old on the streets of Lagos, the Nigerian capital. 'When I was young I always dreamed I'd play in Europe, especially in Germany or England,' he says. 'My father loved football. He encouraged me to play and, when I had the opportunity to go to Europe to further my career, he gave me the finance to go there.'

Timi (his full name is Adewusi Olurotimi) was 17 when a footballing friend put him in touch with an agent. 'The agent made me a lot of promises before I left Nigeria; and because I was only a teenager I had to sign lots of papers for my parents saying that he was going to take care of me and find me a club. He said that if I came to Europe I would live better than in Nigeria, play good football, be happy, gain a lot of money and play in a big club. I believed him.'

What happened next was just one example of a football scandal that is now being investigated at the highest levels of the United Nations. It is a story that stretches from the slums of Rio to the shanty towns of Soweto; a seedy, frightening saga of human trafficking and exploitation that borders on slavery. How it could happen at the dawn of the twenty-first century is testimony to the greed and opportunism of much of the modern game.

Timi's agent touted him around clubs in Austria, Germany, Denmark and Croatia, but each time, a deal fell through. Finally, they had a dispute and the teenager found himself homeless and friendless on the streets of Vienna in the depths of an Austrian winter. He sought refuge at the Celestial Church of Christ.

'They helped me because they thought that with nowhere to stay I might die. But there was a problem with some other young guys who were selling drugs and everyone got thrown out. There was no place for me to go. I didn't know anybody. In the night if I wanted to sleep, I went inside a bus. It was so cold.'

After a fortnight of sleeping rough and scrounging for food, Timi managed to contact a friend and fellow footballer in the Belgian city of Antwerp. 'He said if I could get to Belgium I could stay with him for a while and from there I could get a club. I came through in the back of a truck. My visa was almost finished. I stayed with my friend for a while and sometimes I went to the park to train to keep fit.'

Eventually Timi's friend arranged for a team manager to watch him train. The man was impressed and Timi now plays for a Belgian second-division side. He says his papers are in order and he is getting paid. If his case were an isolated one, it could be explained away as just one of those things that happens in sport. But his story is one of many.

In 1999, in her annual report to the United Nations Commission on Human Rights, the Special Rapporteur for children's rights criticized the world of football for what was, in effect, human trafficking. Ofelia Calcetas-Santos, a lawyer from the Philippines, wrote:

Head-hunters scout in certain countries, notably in Africa, looking for potential star athletes, give their parents or guardians money and then bring the boys to other countries, especially in northern Europe, to be offered to different football teams.

The problem arises when no team will take the boy, who is then usually abandoned and left to fend for himself.

As the UN pointed out, most of the victims were African. Ironically, what had opened up their continent for unscrupulous talent-spotters were the great strides its players made on the world football scene. The breakthrough came when Cameroon, the 'Indomitable Lions', reached the quarter-finals of Italia 90 and nearly brought England's campaign to a halt. The following decade saw African stars finally make an impact in Europe. In 1995, Milan striker George Weah became the first to be voted European Footballer of the Year. A year later, Nigeria won gold at the Olympic Games.

But while European fans were enjoying the excitement that African players were bringing to the game, a small but dubious band of middlemen were beginning to scour the football pitches of Lagos, Accra, Addis Ababa and elsewhere for talent they could sell to the rich clubs of the West. Some worked as official or unofficial scouts for legitimate agents; others were little more than vultures. The lure for the players was money and fame. While it would be wrong to suggest that all African footballers come from poverty, few could hope to earn the fortunes available to them in Europe by staying in Africa.

The centre for this new trade in talent was Brussels, the political heart of the European Union, where well-heeled MEPs rub shoulders with tourists sipping Trappist beers in the cafés of the Grand Place. It also has its share of beggars. In the Matonge district, it's not hard to find 16- and 17-year-old footballers who have been left to their fate. Some sell drugs or commit petty crimes in order to feed and clothe themselves.

Alarm bells first rang with a Belgian players' union, the Sport and Freedom Association, in 1997. Its president, Paul Carlier, said: 'What's happening here now is exploitation of the most cruel and blatant kind, a legal minefield and, at the moment, almost impossible to prevent.'

Mr Carlier claims to know of more than 1,000 young players from Africa, South America and eastern Europe who were fooled by promises of contracts that never materialized. One of the worst cases was that of a teenager from Cameroon who was signed to a Belgian third division on a contract written in Dutch, a language he doesn't understand. It tied him to the club for no fixed wage.

'They slipped me £10 or £15 when they felt like it, here and there,' he later told the *Guardian*. 'I played for them like that all season.' Then in May 1997 an agent offered him a deal at a first division club. He says he signed an agreement to give the agent five per cent of his earnings; a nought was later written in after the five, making it 50 per cent.

Sport and Freedom took its concerns to Pag-Asa, an organization which shelters victims of human trafficking. From its ramshackle office in a graffiti-scarred Brussels back street, it mainly helps victims of prostitution rings, but on the day that *On The Line* visited it was trying to find beds for fifty illegal Albanian refugees who had just been caught by the police. Other typical clients include domestic workers for diplomats and labourers in textile sweatshops.

Pag-Asa co-ordinator Johan Witters says: 'Sport and Freedom asked us if this had something to do with human trades. It became clear that what was happening with these young guys was basically the same as what happened with young prostitutes and with other young foreigners in difficulties.

'The first story we heard was about a young boy out of Cameroon who was recruited by a manager (in Europe, confusingly, a "manager" is an agent) in his own country, someone who just went there scouting young football players. The manager must have thought that the guy was talented because he presented him with a contract. But one of the conditions was that he had to pay half of his salary to the manager for life – plus all the costs for bringing him to Belgium and for giving him lodging, food, whatever. In fact, when you read this contract, which was illegal, the player had to play for the profit of the manager without keeping anything from himself.

'They do not realize what they are signing. They are starting from life conditions in Africa, and have no idea about the cost of living in western Europe. It is clear that the agents abuse the fact that the young African players are not aware of conditions in Europe. Most of them know the African mentality, they know football and know there is a market for those kind of players here in Belgium. They are using their knowledge to mislead young African players by giving them perspectives which can never be realized once the guys are here. They do the job for other official agents who have licences.'

Those who do not make the grade are often simply abandoned: 'We found some in a small room above a bar, four or five boys in one room just illegally dumped there. From time to time we hear stories of boys who played in first- and second-division clubs who were noted on the referee lists even though their identity has never been checked. I cannot imagine that the clubs and leagues are unaware of this. But when we speak about it they try to deny it.'

Mr Witters knows that this is not just a Belgian problem. 'It's clearly a European problem. Some of the boys we are in touch with speak about other European countries, Austria, Slovakia, Germany, Holland, France.'

One weapon Belgium has in place to combat the exploitation of foreign nationals is the state-funded Centre for Equal Opportunities and Anti-racism, and it was not long before it was alerted. Paul Nits, who specializes in investigating human trafficking for the Centre, found that few of the footballers had been aware of the risks when they agreed to come to Europe. A gaunt, intense man in his forties, with a flowing moustache and an overflowing ashtray, he works in a Brussels office block from behind a desk piled high with papers, reports, statements and folders.

'The recruiters are mostly Belgian,' he says. 'They go to Africa, recruit five young players, and try to sell them to Belgian clubs. If they can sell two of the five, it's good business for them – and the other three are not their problem.'

What is even better business is the commission they get each time if they can keep the players moving from club to club. As Danny Jordaan, chief executive of the South African Football Association, pointed out: 'What other salesman, even of second-hand cars, gets a cut every time his product changes hands?'

With the involvement of the Equal Opportunities Centre, a quasi-governmental body, the media finally began to show an interest in the story. In February 1998 the *International Herald Tribune* ran a piece headlined 'Africa's Soccer Dreamers Neglect to Read the Small Print'. Ghanaian international Charles

Akonnor told the paper he had signed what he thought was a two-year contract with the German club Fortuna Cologne; in fact the contract was for five years. He went to court to seek his release, but lost the case. 'When I signed, I was very young and eager to go to Europe and play,' he said. 'I put all my trust in an agent. I didn't understand the German language.'

A Belgian professor in labour law, Roger Blanpain, added his weight to calls to end the exploitation. Then the Centre for Equal Opportunity published a report devoting four pages to the soccer slaves. It made national news in Belgium. The Belgian FA finally admitted there was a problem and said it was 'trying to make it very difficult for agents to bring young players in unless there was a reasonable chance of them getting a contract'.

The most highly-publicized case in Belgium became that of Bayou Mulu, a midfielder good enough to make the Ethiopian B-team in his teens and voted the best young player in east Africa. He was contacted by a talent scout. 'He wanted to take me to Europe. He promised a lot of things; a contract and money for my family and club,' says Bayou.

The scout was working for well-established European soccer agent who got Bayou trials at several clubs, including Belgian first-division outfit Lokeren.

'I played a match with the reserves and trained with the first team. The trainer was positive about me, then he said they would like to give me a contract, so I was happy. The contract was written in Flemish.'

The problem was, Bayou didn't understand Flemish. He was told the contract was for 18 months, at the minimum wage of about £160 a week, far less money than many of his team-mates were earning. After only five months, Lokeren booted him out. With the help of Pag-Asa he launched legal action. Lokeren secretary André Verbraekken insists the club acted fairly and denies encouraging young players to come to Belgium. However, this is not the message found on the club's official website:

We receive a lot of mail from young players from all over the world who are looking for a career as a professional soccer player for a

European club. As the saying goes: a lot are called but few are chosen. Anyway, we'll try to give talent the best opportunity there is.

After telling prospective players to send in references and a video, it adds:

If it looks interesting, we'll send an invitation to you to participate for a week in the trainings. This means you're paying the flights, we look for a place to stay in Lokeren. Even if Lokeren doesn't need a type of player of your kind at that moment, we'll try to show you to other clubs in Belgium or abroad. Just remember: it's a long, long, hard way to realise this kind of dream. If you succeed, it's paradise.

The agent in the Bayou Mulu saga was Antwerp-based Louis de Vries, a man of good reputation in the football world. He has been established for over 20 years and deals on a regular basis with top clubs like Ajax and Feyenoord. His problems blew up when a Dutch probe into alleged financial irregularities in an unrelated transfer led the authorities to raid his office.

'When the Dutch tax authorities were in Belgium, somebody from the Belgian justice department mentioned that I had been under investigation because of a complaint by the girlfriend of an Ethiopian football player. The player had said that we had brought him to Belgium and had not respected the rules of labour and the rules of immigration,' says Mr de Vries. 'Then the thing started to escalate and I was suddenly accused of being a slave-trader, which is completely outrageous and completely untrue.

'The player signed a contract for 18 months. The fault is with Lokeren because, having signed the player, and the player having been allowed a temporary permit to stay here, Lokeren neglected to get his definitive permit. Then they tried to get rid of the player. We tried to assist him, but he disappeared because he was afraid that he would have to leave the country. We have treated him in a perfect way; have acted according to the laws and rules and spent a lot of money. We paid his hotel and phone bills, gave him money, and made sure he had a proper professional contract. What happened afterwards was not within my responsibilities.'

Mr de Vries insists he is innocent of any wrongdoing, but admits that such trafficking does exist. Despite his protestations, the Antwerp Public Affairs Ministry is investigating. As this book went to press, several other court decisions were pending at the end of 1999, but the Belgian judicial system is notoriously slow.

'I am aware that in this kind of business a lot of things go wrong, but I'm deeply shocked that I was given as an example (of wrongdoing) when the whole country knows who the bad guys are and where people should go to find out about these kind of things,' says Mr de Vries. 'There are people who are specialists in that. They don't respect any laws whatsoever. It's a scandal, it's outrageous, it has been going on for a long time. But, again, the media, football people, club directors and club managers, as well as the police, know who these people are and where to find them. I hope they will do something about it quickly.'

Mr de Vries will not name names. Does he deal with these people? 'No. Absolutely not.'

So who are these middlemen? Sports journalist Jan Antonissen is an expert on Africans playing in Europe, and he says dangerous criminals have become involved in their recruitment. 'You have big-time managers who earn a lot and bring people to top clubs, but you also have small people without licences who go to Africa and sometimes bring or smuggle people into Belgium – I have been told by a lot of African players that these people are also active in the prostitution business. They smuggle girls in the country or – as I have been told – bring in the sisters of the football players as well. It is about football players, prostitutes, crime in general, even drugs and weapons.

'It also happens to Latin Americans and east Europeans - young people who don't have anything to lose and who are eager to gain a lot of money in soccer – I think the main difference between the African and east European players is that the African players are brought here by private initiatives whereas east

European players seem to be brought here by gangs or the mafia.'

The involvement of organized crime groups is perhaps the most worrying aspect of this trade. One agent with a particular influence in Nigeria is believed to be involved in recruiting players' sisters as prostitutes. One Nigerian player had his contract signed by his agent and the club, and didn't even get to sign it himself.

Paul Carlier of Sport and Freedom says, 'Anyone can declare themselves to be an agent. Each has five or six mobile phones, and they spend their lives in aeroplanes. Having picked players like cattle, they buy them for nothing, put them in a club that serves as a showcase and then sell them on for a lot more. Throughout the world of football, groups like ours are encountering massive resistance.'

The Belgian football federation admits it has been partly to blame for not taking action earlier to clean up the game. It is also true that some of the players may be exploiting the situation to stay in Europe illegally, blaming others when they are caught. The Belgians insist the problem is no worse in their country than in many others, but it has attracted more publicity because they are trying to do something about it. New legislation will require contracts to be written in a language the players understand and will double the minimum salary. Paul Nits at the Centre for Equal Opportunity is also pursuing several legal actions.

'The Centre has a right to undertake actions in court and at this moment there are some dossiers in court where we are undertaking actions in the interest of players. The players themselves who are often in Belgium illegally get a permit to stay because they are considered to be victims of trafficking in human beings. They also get shelter and food, the support of social workers, and so on. The action that we take is against the people who are responsible for letting the players come to Belgium without the necessary permits or papers to allow them to stay for a year or more. We also take action against the clubs who exploit young players, who do not pay the player what is set out in the contract that they presented to the administration.'

The set-up in Britain means that it could not happen here. Overseas players from outside the European Community have to be recognized internationals before they can get a work permit. However, fears have been expressed that Premier League clubs could benefit by the back door, through perfectly legitimate tie-ups with foreign sides who could be used to nurture young hopefuls.

Late in 1998, Manchester United, the richest club in the world, struck a deal with Royal Antwerp for the Belgian side to act as a 'feeder' club, allowing United to sign new talent and also to give some of the Reds' home-grown youngsters valuable experience by playing abroad. The deal had an added attraction: 'In Belgium you can get a work permit far more easily than you can in England,' said Royal Antwerp secretary Paul Bistiaux. So, if, after qualifying for Belgian citizenship, a player, initially spotted by United and 'loaned' to Royal Antwerp, is deemed to have made the grade, he will be invited to move to Old Trafford.

United then announced a further deal, with South African First Division club FC Fortune of Cape Town, to develop African youth players in May 1999. It was reported that selected players were to be flown to England to attend trials with a view to being signed by United, although they would not be able to play in England until they had become accepted internationals in their own country. 'We believe this link will give us entry to a rich seam of African football talent and discover players for us to follow in the steps of our academy products such as David Beckham, Ryan Giggs and the Nevilles,' said manager Alex Ferguson.

United director and solicitor Maurice Watkins knew nothing of the human-trade scandal until he was informed by *On The Line*, and was adamant that United would not help to bolster such a system.

'MUFC would not allow its name to be tied to any such matter. We are justifiably proud of our youth policy. We look after our youth players and if any young players were involved in this co-operation their progress would be monitored very carefully. Any co-operation with a Belgian club is not a one-way business, it would be two-way and would also involve young players from MUFC going to the Belgian club for experience in playing on loan in a Belgian team.'

Mr Watkins promises the club will act if it ever finds its name was being misused by unlicensed agents to entice young players. 'We would take every action necessary to stop our name being used in that way. Manchester United only deals with licensed agents. This is a FIFA requirement.'

Not only is the Belgian Federation is trying to stop agents bringing in young players unless there is a reasonable chance of them getting a contract but, more importantly on-going criminal investigations could result in fines or even jail terms for the guilty. But that's only in Belgium. In Germany, a Ghanaian international recently claimed he thought his five-year contract was only for two years. And Egyptian star Hossam Hassan left a Swiss club after complaining that he had not really understood the deal he signed.

Until being unseated in the 1999 Euro elections, Tony Cunningham was a British MEP who took up the fight for soccer slaves. A former football coach in Africa and a Labour Party spokesman on Third World issues, he was well-placed to raise the matter at the highest levels. He admits, 'If you are a young footballer, living in Uganda or the slums of Rio de Janeiro and someone comes along and promises you a house, a car and lots of money, of course you are going to jump at the opportunity. But the reality for many of these young footballers is that they don't make the grade and end up in unhappy circumstances, and basically thoroughly exploited.

'For the five, six or even ten million pounds a club would spend on a striker, you could afford to bring in 200-300 African kids and if one of them makes it then you can save the money. The problem, of course, are the ones that don't make it.'

Mr Cunningham has fought for justice for young players with the European Parliament and football authorities. He extracted a promise from Marcus Studer, deputy general secretary of UEFA, that: 'UEFA will carefully examine this problem and, together with FIFA, try to find solutions and take appropriate measures. However, as you certainly know, the possibilities for the governing bodies of sports organizations to act are currently limited'.

In correspondence, Mr Studer says the Bosman ruling of December 1995 and the abolition of restrictions on EC players by the European Court of Justice, had transformed the football map:

As a consequence of this decision, foreign players have 'invaded' professional clubs [in] Europe's various football leagues. Squads with eleven foreign players are becoming increasingly commonplace. Moreover, young and talented players from South America and Africa are joining European clubs in the hope of playing in the first team. However, their chances of doing so are very limited, because experienced and long-serving players are already occupying these positions on the pitch. Therefore, only the best of these young players really have a chance to fulfil the requirements of a club and to have their contracts renewed. The others will unfortunately lose their jobs. We agree that football's authorities, as well as the political authorities, should exercise their responsibilities to find ways to protect such young players.

UEFA is already trying to set up a new model contract to protect the players as well as the clubs. In accordance with the specific national labour law, such a contract should then be recommended to our member associations for implementation. We have therefore already contacted the International Players' Association FIFPRo, and they are involved in a working group to fund a common agreement on such a model contract. This contract will also contain a special clause for young players, which will allow the player to attend school or other educational programmes. We hope that such a model contract will then also be authorized by the various national and international authorities.

Despite such assurances, the brutal truth is that as long as there are vast inequalities in wealth, and football offers one of the few means of escape, the scandal of soccer slavery will continue in some form. As Johan Witters of Pag-Asa says, 'I can imagine that for an African player it is really good to know that one day he might be a famous player in any European country. It is a dream – and for many it will ever stay a dream.'

CHAPTER ELEVEN

Piranhas Among Minnows
The Hooligans Moving in on Non-league Soccer

A quiet, inviting pub in County Durham seems an unlikely sort of meeting place for some of Britain's most notorious football hooligans. But that's where the self-styled 'Misfits', who follow Tow Law Town of the Arnott Insurance Northern League, spend the cold, winter evenings.

The former mining town of Tow Law – which sits on the top of the Pennines, 40 miles from Newcastle, suffered more than most due to the decline of Britain's mining industry in the 1980s. The club's biggest claim to fame is that Chris Waddle started his career at Ironworks Lane, Tow Law's home, which was once described as the nearest football ground to the moon.

In 1998 Tow Law Town got to Wembley, eventually losing in the final of the FA Vase, to Tiverton Town, and their route to the twin towers took them outside their usual north-east stamping ground. Wherever the team went, the 'Misfits' followed – and they have not been forgotten by the officials of the clubs they visited. What is especially worrying for the football authorities is the fact that the 'Misfits' are just the tip of the iceberg. Now that football fans are being priced out of being able to support high-profile teams, many see the cuddly non-League game as the obvious place to cause trouble.

A Saturday lunchtime meeting with the Misfits was arranged. We met in the pub's games room and were introduced to several members including brothers Paul and Simon. They took us to their mother's home where they both live, they were chatty and amiable, and obviously proud of their town and football club.

Unfortunately neither the town of Tow Law nor its football

team share those feelings, hence the name of the group – 'Misfits'. They number up to 40 in their ranks and admit they have been brought up in a tough environment where fighting and standing up for your mates is almost second nature.

The club has made every effort to disassociate themselves from the Misfits but, despite this, Simon loyally insists they will carry on following their team. ' We are not really welcome up there because we're not part of their system. They don't want us, so we called ourselves Misfits. We're their unofficial supporters.'

They cheerfully show off cuttings detailing their exploits, including photographs of the group in France for the 1998 World Cup, and happily relive stories of their battles around football's lesser-known outposts. Perhaps most strikingly – and a sure sign that the mentality of the big-time hooligan is creeping into non-League games – is the calling cards they showed us: *Tow Law Misfits, Non-League Football Hooligans – you've met the rest now meet the best'*, one boasted, another read: *Don't be a mug, be a Tow Law thug*.

The sort of publicity the Misfits attract is decidedly unwelcome for John Flynn, a softly spoken solicitor from nearby Consett, who is also the chairman of the Tow Law. The club feels that it has done everything it can to stop this particular brand of travelling support. 'We were able to notify the local police of the coach company that the official supporters were travelling with, and able to give them the number plates for those coaches, so any unofficial supporters could be identified.'

For Tow Law, the road to Wembley in 1997 started well. In the second round, the club travelled to the foothills of east Lancashire to face Rossendale United at Dark Lane. For Jack Feber, Rossendale's chairman, 'segregation', 'stewarding' and 'security', were not words that usually cropped up for the average crowd of 120, but they certainly came into use when the Misfits came to town.

'Our secretary got a phone call saying there could be trouble, but we didn't expect anything like what we got – they were hooligans, just hooligans who went on the rampage as soon as they arrived. I think most of them were intoxicated – had had enough beer before they even got here. They caused havoc in the Boars Head, throwing glasses about, using abusive language, then they arrived on our ground and made a beeline for the social club. ' It weren't long before they were throwing glasses. They also broke numerous pictures off the walls, set off fire extinguishers, and ripped up the snooker table.'

Unfortunately this affray proved to be far from an isolated incident. As Tow Law got closer to Wembley, the Misfits caused more and more havoc. In the fifth round when the club played Sudbury Town of the Jewson Counties Eastern League there were more problems. Tow Law won 2-1, their reward, a trip back to Sudbury to play the town's other team, the Wanderers. According to Brian Tatum, the Wanderers' club secretary, by the time the draw was made, he was fully aware of the Misfits' reputation.

'We knew because we all share an interest in the FA Vase and knew of trouble at Rossendale. We saw they were drawn against Sudbury Town who didn't seem to take any great pre-cautions. They caused alarm among market stall holders and causing problems with townspeople. When they got to the ground, because they had kept the bar open, there were further problems. They got on the pitch when Tow Law scored. A number dropped their trousers and exposed themselves to the crowd, and were generally being a thoroughly bad nuisance. We were forewarned by local police that they had been around pubs and left calling cards which said they were the Tow Law Misfits, you've met the rest, now meet the best.'

The game ended one goal each which meant Sudbury making the long trip to the North East for the replay. According to Brian Tatum, as soon as the Sudbury coach pulled into Tow Law things got ugly.

'As you go in, the road goes round a bend and there is a pub from which you can see the road. By the time our coach turned the corner, about a dozen lads had stormed out of the pub and there was an array of bottles and glass rattling against the side of the coach. We had youngsters there who were terrified by this. The police told the coach driver not to leave it anywhere near the ground. In fact, the driver took the coach 3-4 miles out of Tow Law to another small village and got a taxi back to Tow Law for which we said we would reimburse him because we all felt safer with the coach out of danger.'

For Mr Tatum there is only one way to describe them:

'Thugs – absolute thugs. They're not interested in the football. All they want to do is go out, get boozed up and have a good scrap.'

There is no doubt that the 'Tow Law Misfits' deserve their reputation as one of non-League football's least welcome visitors. But a search through the surprisingly professional web sites dedicated to non-League football teams soon reveals that crowd trouble at football matches is by no means confined to the Premiership or Football League. Ask any non-League football fan whether hooliganism is a problem and they will form a defence as well marshalled as any seen on the pitch.

The reason that non-League games are so popular is that they offer supporters the chance to watch football without any of the baggage that goes with League-level games. Non-League games are cheap, safe and friendly and, for those very reasons, their football fans are incredibly protective of them. According to Misfit Simon, there are also reasons why it is attractive to football followers like him: 'You can't get in most Premiership clubs, so people who are disillusioned follow their local sides instead. When you've got a team like Tow Law who do well going to Wembley, you get a good following who jump on the bandwagon ... Obviously there are lads following the other side as well, so then when you're all full of drink it ends up in a pitched battle.'

Simon told us that when Tow Law did get to Wembley the Misfits marked their trip to London by causing more trouble:

'There was a bit of trouble in a pub called The Globe... All hell was let loose in there, chairs, bottles, glasses, the lot went flying. We were outnumbered totally by the Tiverton lot, but I am sure we came out on top at the end.'

The next season Tow Law sought to make up for its Wembley failure, and in the second round were drawn away to former League club Workington. At the time, the Cumbrians were entertaining Ramsbottom and Prescott Cables in the North Western Trains League at their Borough Park ground, which, in its hey-day, once saw the likes of the world famous 'Busby Babes'.

The Misfits were ready for trouble, but thanks to a phone call from Rossendale United, the home club was also prepared. Predictably, Simon claims the Misfits were not to blame.

'The police were heavy handed, pushing us all over the street... We were walking round the streets singing Tow Law songs, and they didn't like it. It wasn't really our fault... They started the trouble in the ground. Two of our lads went to the toilet just before half time, and got jumped by their lads, so our lads ran in. That's they way it works. There's nothing else we could do. We had to back our lads up.'

On this occasion the consequences were far more serious for the Misfits: four of their group were arrested and – after an enforced extended stay on the West Cumbrian coast – appeared at the local magistrates court. The FA took such a dim view of these events that it ordered an immediate enquiry. Yet more notoriety for the Tow Law Misfits.

The overall responsibility for policing football in Britain falls at the door of Assistant Chief Constable Tim Hollis. He recognizes that many football fans relish the opportunity to cause trouble at non-League grounds because they resemble the League grounds of the 'bad old days' of the 1970s and 1980s.

'As there has been improved stewarding, better control, better safety issues at the top level of the game, with all-seater stadia, closed circuit television, and more stewards, there's no doubt some of the trouble has been displaced. If only 20 people are misbehaving in a total of 70 people, it's not a small problem, it's a very significant one.'

On their calling cards the Misfits also claim to be linked to an infamously violent group called 'the Gremlins' who follow Newcastle United. John Williams of the respected

Norman Chester Centre for Football Research at Leicester University thinks the problem goes a step further with hooligans from League clubs using the non-League game to confront rivals.

'It's certainly true that some people who have been in trouble at larger clubs also have their local community gangs, and supporters are often drawn from places that have non-League teams. Now when these non-League teams play each other, it provides a perfect opportunity for locally based gangs who also support large Premier League clubs to act out this Premier League rivalry at a meeting between smaller non-League clubs. All the same attractions are there: it's open, there's less policing and more opportunity for action. Certainly there are occasions when you see supporters of Premier League clubs fighting at non-League matches.'

This is certainly what happened at a game involving Gresley Rovers of the Dr Martens League. Robert, a Gloucester City fan, visited the Derbyshire club to watch his side play.

'Basically it was a full-scale riot and the Gloucester fans were totally unprepared for violence on this scale. The fighting carried on for a good quarter-of-an hour spilling out on to the pitch. Eventually, the police turned up and several of the Gresley fans were led away. The police told us that, in their opinion, they were locally- based Derby County fans who had come along to the Gresley game because they wanted to have a go at the Gloucester fans.'

In their book *Capital Punishment* (Headline), Dougie and Eddie Brimson – authors of several books on football hooliganism, who usually follow Watford – devote a chapter to the attraction of the non-League game, documenting many incidents involving teams from the lower leagues:

For many experienced hooligans, the opportunity to play up at a ground where the stewards and the police have no idea what to expect is something that is too good to miss. The fact that there will almost certainly be no CCTV in place to film them is an added bonus. It must be said that these people are highly unlikely to be

*regular supporters at the club but unfortunately for the team con-
cerned, this image is likely to stick. And when the next big game
comes along the opposition will have their following turn out and
the whole thing starts to snowball.*

The non-League game, according to the Brimson brothers, has
its fair share of hooligans. Stevenage Borough 'had a fair little
mob'; a group from Woking took on Millwall fans after an FA
Cup game; Tooting and Mitcham followers caused some
trouble which resulted in an opposing manager having to stop
one pitch-invader using a corner flag as a javelin. They also cite
trouble at Canvey Island, Boreham Wood and Tilbury – not traditional hot-beds of football, but all clubs that have found their
way on to the hooligan map.

There is no doubt that the well organized hooligan element of League and Premiership team-followers, with their
individual gang identities, is now creeping into the non-
Leagues. Robert is probably one of the few die hard non-League
fans who is prepared to admit that there is a problem in the
non-League game. As mentioned before, many fans who follow
teams, such as Frickley Athletic and Taunton Town, find it hard
to accept that their particular clubs might harbour a violent
following.

Lansdowne Road, Dublin, in 1995 remains one of English
football's worst nights. The international friendly against the
Republic of Ireland was abandoned half way through the first
half after English followers rioted on the terraces. Labour Euro
MP Glyn Ford a long-time campaigner against racism was
watching the match on television. He immediately phoned the
anti-fascist group Searchlight.

'They looked at the footage and identified a number of
people from BNP, I think from the National Front, Combat 18
and Column 88 – all extreme right-wing groups. Also from a
group called the Cheltenham Volunteer Force based primarily
in Cheltenham, and I understand that some of these same
people have been involved in trouble at Cheltenham.'

It is alleged that the CVF – who were linked to Football

League newcomers Cheltenham Town – did have ties with neo-nazi groups which are close to being terrorist groups, an allegation that, according to Mr Ford, has never been challenged.

This is obviously a worrying trend for the non-League game – and one that was not helped by the supporters of Yeovil Town of the Conference which faced Cardiff City in a tense FA Cup tie in 1998, and displayed a Protestant terrorist Red Hand of Ulster flag. This led to a protest by the Welsh clubs chaplain and an apology by the Yeovil Chairman.

The link between football and right-wing groups is well documented, but, according to Glynn Ford, it reached bizarre proportions in Manchester in the 1970s when: 'There was an actual National Front football team in the local Leagues. That particular issues was very difficult to deal with when you are playing against them. It would have been extremely difficult for black players to play against a team that were overtly racist."

Fortunately the team did not stay in the League for long after numerous incidents of trouble, which required police intervention.

The chance to appear on a bigger stage is an obvious attraction for the followers of low-profile sides in the lower leagues, and this goes some way to explain why international away-matches are such a magnet. According to one non-League fan (who goes under the name of Captain B): 'I know of a group who plagued the World Cup, but who came back with contacts made about which matches would be worth visiting in the Dr Martens League. Strange thing is a lot of these people are not just big-game boys. When violence kicks off, there are a lot of "ordinary fans" who are only too happy to join the affray.'

As France '98 proved, football fans are under almost constant surveillance by the National Criminal Intelligence Service (NCIS), but it does not collate information on non-League teams. Glyn Ford thinks this is something the NCIS should definitely be thinking seriously about.

'I wouldn't want to see them being too heavy handed, but we need an appropriate response. It would be sensible for the NCIS to look at what is happening at some non-League grounds and to start collecting information. Then, if the trouble spreads, they should put in some more resources. There is no reason why NCIS information should not be circulated to non-League grounds where there are trouble-makers. Some of these people are actually banned from League grounds which is exactly why they go to non-League ones.'

Ken Marsden is the Chairman of the Unibond League, the next level down on the non-League pyramid from the Conference. He reluctantly admits that there is a problem at his level of the game.

'Yes, some clubs do have this element who follow them around. It is not every match; it is usually high-profile matches, either cup matches or end-of-season championship matches which produce this element.'

The winners of the Unibond League in 1999 were Altrincham, who play just down the road from Old Trafford and Maine Road. At times over the years this club has stepped gloriously but briefly out of the shadow of its more illustrious neighbours as one of cup football's most famous giant-killers. In March 1997, though, the club faced a fairly routine FA Trophy game against Bishop Auckland at it home-ground Moss Lane. For Gerry Berman, the Altrincham chairman, the match proved to be one of the worst in his memory.

The police were forced to stop the match for 20 minutes after some Bishop Auckland followers rioted. According to Mr Berman, the travelling supporters had been drinking from early afternoon and had caused trouble in the town centre. The police reportedly faced chants of ' Let's get the Pigs' and finally the violence got so bad in the ground that special officers had to be brought in from a home game at nearby Manchester United.

As with the incident involving followers of Tow Law and Workington, the FA launched an inquiry. But, according to Gerry Berman, there were unusual circumstances behind the trouble:

'One of our players, George Shepherd, who we had signed from Macclesfield Town had broken his leg and he won a legal fight against Bishop Auckland and received several thousand pounds. So there was an incitement before the game started.

Gerry Berman, though, is only too aware of the problem for non-League clubs who may only get 200-300 paying spectators per game. 'It costs £250 for a policeman. I don't know what the charge is for a dog or a horse. You multiply that a few times and your profits have gone from the game. We don't want policeman at the ground, we're well stewarded and the stewards are trained, but if it's a big game we realize that there has to be a minimal amount of police there for law and order.'

Ken Marsden, chairman of the League, agrees that many clubs who do not have the finances to employ adequate stewards rely on the good will of loyal fans. 'I suspect that in a lot of places club stewards are not properly trained, but this can be easily remedied. The police run courses and a lot of clubs do take advantage of this. When stewards are well trained, they do have an effect. Policing is expensive at really out-of-the-way non-League clubs, but in high-profile games it's a necessity for the safety of the public.'

For many clubs the spectre of racism at football games, a by-product of the 1970s and 1980s, has all but been removed. The idea that a local league in multi-cultural Manchester would now entertain a team made up of National Front members is ludicrous and would be comical, too, if it was not so disturbing. But unfortunately the non-League game has one club in its ranks which still has a racist problem on its terraces.

Tucked away on the flatlands of Lincolnshire, Wisbech Town of the Dr Martens League, came to notoriety when England centre forward Les Ferdinand spoke to the BBC's *On Side* about his time in the non-League game. When asked about racist abuse in the game he admitted that worst he had come across was in the non-Leagues at Wisbech, which he admitted nearly put him off playing football for life.

Another player who has encountered the fans at Wisbech is Leroy Rosenior, a centre forward with West Ham, Charlton and Bristol City. He remembers going to Wisbech with Gloucester City in 1997 and being astonished at what he heard from the terraces.

'It wasn't just a few people, it was a lot of the crowd. It seemed to be the norm which is very disturbing and went on all through the game. In fact, one supporter came up and apologized to me and Adie Ming, who was in my side then, for the amount of abuse we received.'

After many years playing the game at the highest level at some of English football's most intimidating grounds, it is perhaps a surprise that Rosenior should find the following quote noteworthy.

'When I first started playing, I had a lot of problems at certain clubs in the League, but it wasn't scary because there were thousands and thousands of people and you couldn't actually see their faces or the hate in their eyes. It wasn't as disturbing as seeing someone trying to get over the barrier, and not being quite sure what he wanted to do with you. So, in that sense, when there were fewer people it was actually scarier. It didn't happen that often, but when it did it was more extreme.'

For Robert, a Gloucester fan, his trip to the Fenlands to watch the game was something quite surreal. ' The Wisbech game was quite incredible. It was like something out of a different world, some sort of bizarre 1970s documentary. It was like going back through time. At the time Gloucester were managed by Leroy Rosenior and we also had several black guys in the side. Unfortunately, a group of about 20 men who came and stood by us took exception to this and their chanting was totally sickening. It was overt neo-fascist abuse. It was quite incredible.'

The club's notoriety is such that in the House of Commons in April 1999, MP Simon Burns spoke of Wisbech fans throwing bananas at Fulham's Barry Hayles when he played there in a cup-tie for Bristol Rovers.

The Wisbech club says it has had problems with racism in the past, but, having banned certain fans, the problem has now been eradicated.

It is only fair to add that the majority of clubs in the non-Leagues have little or no trouble at their matches and the small number of fans who may follow their team to an away-match do strike up friendly relationships with their opposite numbers.

One major problem, according to John Williams of Leicester University, is that since 'one up one down' from the Football League to the Conference was introduced, the bigger clubs have a lot to prove 'We have had fans of clubs from the Football League relegated for the first time going to places which are new, travelling with some status, wanting to demonstrate they're the League club and we can teach non-League supporters a thing or two, and finding that the scene is much more open than the Football League scene. There have been signs that some supporters of Football League clubs have gone down with a view to teaching the non-Leaguers a lesson and demonstrating that fan relations in the Football League are a different thing altogether.'

For clubs like Halifax Town, Doncaster and Hereford which have had long if not entirely successful tenures at the wrong end of the Football League, there is a need to prove their superiority over the lesser lights of non-League football.

The fans of Halifax – now restored to the League after winning the Conference in 1998 – were involved in ugly scenes at Cheltenham where they fought with home fans and caused damage to the stand. The club carried with it a reputation as one of the Conference's nastiest group of followers, and Hereford – which lost its League status on the last day of the season – has also gained notoriety through a group called the 'Hereford Loyalists'.

Doncaster Rovers was relegated to the Conference, and had their chairman, Ken Richardson, jailed after the main stand was burnt down. The club then spent its first season in the non-League languishing at the foot of the table. If things couldn't get much worse, a group of fans who call themselves the DDR or Doncaster Defence Regiment caused a lot of trouble at a lot of grounds. When they played Cheltenham, objects were thrown on the field and towards opposition fans. They also caused trouble in a pub before the game in Woking, and were responsible for several other incidents.

But there is evidence that a local derby or high-profile cup match run will be met with the same passion as any game in the Football League. For example, the first recorded use of CS Gas by police at a football match was not in a high-profile Premiership clash, but in a FA Cup tie between non-League Ilkeston Town and Scunthorpe. On this occasion four people were arrested during fighting involving around 60 fans. A Grantham and Nuneaton Borough match saw one of the most disturbing incidents when two men in the main stand were stabbed by visiting supporters.

Incidents like these, if we are to believe the authorities, have been all but wiped out in senior football in this country, but if you spend time on the web sites that committed fans dedicate even to the most obscure non-League teams then the depth of the problem becomes clear. Stories of reported violence around the lesser-known football grounds are far more widespread than anyone would think or those involved in the non-League game are possibly willing to concede.

In a game between Boston United and Grantham three arrests were made after fighting in the ground. In another match, involving Boston this time against Gainsborough, bottles were thrown at the Gainsborough keeper. Altrincham fans talk of trouble involving Northwich, Barrow, Southport, Morecambe and Witton.

There have also been reports of players from one club in the Dr Martens League shouting racist abuse – a charge which is by no means particular to this club.

One fan of a non-League club described the trouble at a game involving Grantham and Goole as a ' real bona fide riot'.

Kings Lynn was named as having one of the most unpopular groups of supporters. Local rivalries are very common: Merthyr and Barry Town fans clashed during one game; and Nuneaton Borough was involved in fighting Kettering with whom they have had a long-standing rivalry. In the latter instance, many people blamed the problems on a lack of segregation.

It is not just the higher reaches of the pyramid that have violent followers, there were clashes in a game between Leighton Town and Aldershot, and ten of the 3rd Division of the Diadora League. The violence described by one fan was so bad that he said he had never been so petrified in his entire life; and an Aldershot fan was stabbed while 200 or so fans fought pitch battles.

Fans were forced on to the pitch after fighting broke out involving Stevenage Borough and Rushden and Diamonds fans, and this occurred after a policeman reportedly admitted to a fan that segregation was not working.

The unofficial Internet site of Gloucester City of the Dr Martens League has a section called 'Thugs, Lies and Tickertape' devoted to stories of violence. Like many of the clubs its violent followers carry a nickname, in this case the 'City Disorder Boys'. The site has numerous examples of the trouble involving their clubs.

The evidence for those in the non-League game who have been accused of burying their head in the sand is clear: fans at non-League level – fans who have been displaced from League games by the rising cost of ticket prices – are adopting the roles that hooligans play at League level. And hooligans who have been forced into attending non-League games because of the tighter security at League matches are now dragging the non-League game down.

There is also evidence that hooligans from the non-League game are active on the international scene, but, like the clubs that make up the non-League, the police have limited resources to deal with the problem. 'It's a question of degree,' says Tim Hollis of the National Criminal Intelligence Service, ' we have to make judgements. There are ninety-two Premier and Football League clubs and a network of football intelligence officers. If we start saying let's look at the Conference and other clubs, the demand would be substantial.'

For those who dedicate their lives to the non-League game, with no tangible financial rewards, the current state of affairs is very sad. Brian Tatum of Sudbury Wanderers, victims of the Tow Law Misfits, can only look over his small friendly ground and despair. 'At non-League football at our level, the biggest gates are 200-300 people. We mix together, sit together in the stands, meet in the bar afterwards, have a damn good crack about the game and everybody shakes hands. This is what amateur football – or non-League football – is all about. So why these hooligans have attached themselves to non-League football is beyond me. The quicker they are put away the better, in my opinion.'

CHAPTER TWELVE

Boys from the Blacklist
The Innocent Fans Listed as Thugs on Police Databases

Fifteen years after the Heysel tragedy, the reputation of English fans in European competition still goes before them. Manchester United, Arsenal and Chelsea have all won trophies since the ban on English teams playing in Europe was lifted. But for the fans who follow their teams, the return to European competition has not been as successful.

The clubs riding on the success on the field have penalized supporters off it, incurring the wrath of the competition authorities and causing anger, misery and mistrust within the fans. They have denied supporters who have not bought all-inclusive packages the opportunity to travel and buy match tickets independently, and have done this with the full support of the FA.

Ole Gunnar Solksjaer's last-minute winner against Bayern Munich in Barcelona in the 1999 European Cup Final was the greatest moment in Manchester United's history. It was, though, the quarter-final victory over Inter Milan which proved to be the crucial game

According to Adam Brown of United's Independent Supporters' club, fans hoping to travel to Milan were told by the club that there would only be a limited number of tickets on sale for a stadium that held 80,000 people. It was well known, he claims, that around 10,000 United fans planned to make the trip to Italy. Adam Brown's experience on the night are in common with thousands of other British fans who follow their teams to the less glamorous and more obscure football outposts in search of European glory.

Brown tells of tickets sold on the black market for

exorbitant prices; of being directed from the turnstile indicated on the ticket to a busier entrance where there was potentially a crush situation. Once they succeeded in getting into the stadium, they were subjected to a barrage of missiles from the Inter fans after being directed to a different section of the ground. The situation was then made worse, he says, by the actions of the Italian police who, having failed to act when there was a build-up of fans at the front of a queue, which they had helped to create, started... 'Attacking and batoning fans at the front of the crush to get them over the barrier which they had no control and for which the fans were entirely innocent.'

In a report to the Football Supporters Association Adam Brown concludes that: 'Attitudes to travelling English fans must change and change drastically or this will not be the last event of this kind.'

He also gave this stark warning to the football authorities: 'Unless the Football Association listens to what its fans organizations are advising them, involve them fully in the planning for travelling to European matches and respond effectively to problems when they arise, they will continue to be partly culpable for events that happen on other shores.'

Since the reintroduction of the English teams, it has been Manchester United who has been England's most successful team. It won the European Cup Winners Cup in 1991 and had the famous triumph in Barcelona eight years later. The team has, though, faltered along the way. In 1993 it went to Istanbul to play Galatasaray in the Champions League and lost 2-1. Six United fans were detained in Turkey as trouble flared in and outside the ground.

That match proved to be turning point for travelling fans as clubs began to refuse to sell tickets to what are described as 'unofficial fans on unofficial trips'. The Football Supporters Association was less than impressed by this and asked the FA for clarification

The FA's Chief Executive at the time was Graham Kelly, who issued the following statement:

Having been made aware of various problems experienced by supporters of clubs playing in European competitions in season 93/94 the clubs had unanimously decided that tickets should be restricted to supporters travelling on official trips, which as you know is a practice we thoroughly endorse.

Adrian Titcombe, the FA's head of security, summed up the concerns about supporters abroad: 'The incident in Istanbul brought home the point we are trying to make, that it's not really the English hooligan that we're concerned about, it's the fact that innocent groups of English supporters can end up in the wrong place at the wrong time.'

In a statement, the Turkish authorities laid the blame for the incident in Istanbul firmly at the door of the unofficial travelling fans. Andy Thomas, a United follower, remembers though that the majority of incidents were due to heavy handedness by the local police.

'Very quickly people recognized that this was not hooliganism, it was foreign police victimizing a group of people. But after that statement the club still said this incident means that fans must travel with us. But the official trip coaches were stoned; people were hit with missiles; seats were taken by police, many people were not allowed inside, and those that were, were beaten on the way in. Very quickly there was an official line that was used and then taken back, but still that line was used to give clubs a monopoly on travel for whatever reason.'

The options for fans wanting to travel to watch their team are therefore limited: either they go with the official club trip or stay at home and follow the game on radio or television. The packages resemble long-distant hit squads - fans rushed into the town just before the game and then quickly whisked away afterwards, with no time to take in the sights and sounds of the place they are visiting or have a sociable and peaceful drink.

Andy Mitten, the editor of Manchester United's fanzine 'United we Stand', thinks that if fans are paying to support a club they should be allowed to have a say in what they do.

'If you're spending £300 to £400 you just don't want to fly

in, watch the game and fly out. You want to sample the delights that a foreign city can offer.'

A government regulator, already well known to the football authorities, took up the fan's case. The Office of Fair Trading, which took on the Premier League over its television deal in 1999, stepped in on the basis that the policy of clubs selling tickets only to those who buy travel packages, was a restraint of trade. Adrian Titcombe and the Football Association were forced to think again.

'We certainly were suggesting that in the past, but it's been put to us that this may have been against the OFT regulations, so we no longer say that. However, we do support the clear consensus of clubs to control the movement of supporters.'

But in a letter to clubs, the FA continued to support the policy of linking tickets and travel.

This is concerned with tied-in sales, where one product's availability is dependent upon the customer buying another product as well. Expressed simply in football terms, it means you cannot have a seat at the game if you do not get a seat on the plane.

Not so long ago – in fact even more recently than their European Cup winning days under Brian Clough – Nottingham Forest's fans were planning trips to Europe's far-flung football outposts. At that time, according to Dave Pullen, the club's then-Commercial Manager, the club was making a loss on the trips it ran abroad.

'If we're talking about the clubs making vast sums of money from the tips abroad, then that is simply untrue. If we take into account the cost of the dummy-runs that have to be performed prior to the tie taking place to try and see that everything runs smoothly, I would suggest that we are not making a profit at all.'

It is the same story from other clubs. They treat the away-leg of a European tie as a loss-limitation exercise rather than a profit-making one, a strange anathema in today's ultra-commercial age.

When Alan Roberts was Leeds United's General Manager, he showed the sums to the Office of Fair Trading in order to illustrate the 'break-even policy'. He agrees with Dave Pullen at Forest: 'I've produced figures on this and, like most clubs, we have not made any money. The intention is not to make profit on the away-leg. Profit doesn't come into it. You make your money on the home-leg.'

Football found itself in a quandary because of the suggestion of monopoly abuse. What the OFT regards as a fair trading issue is seen by the Football Association as a threat to safety. Adrian Titcombe, the safety officer at Lancaster Gate, says his priority is the fans. 'We have to make sure there is minimal trouble associated with English clubs abroad and if there is any other legislation which impedes us from doing this then we have to be concerned.'

Titcombe then issued a warning to all English fans who loyally follow their team: 'We must face the facts that we are not starting with a blank sheet of paper. If there are incidents involving English fans abroad, the initial reaction will be to blame the English. If we have too many incidents, there is the possibility of another ban.'

The message from the FA is clear enough, but incidents like Galatasaray in 1993 obviously suited clubs and justified them keeping travel to European games 'in house', even though the evidence pointed to the English fans being innocent.

Adrian Titcombe says that the clubs have to be cautious: 'Clearly some people may argue that they are trying to take unfair advantage of the situation, but certainly all the discussions I have had, have centred on the very real danger of incidents jeopardizing English football abroad.'

The question of safety for the thousands of English fans who are simply intent on supporting their teams, came to the attention of Euro MP and football fan Glyn Ford. He was fully aware of how the current feelings on the Continent favoured English clubs as opposed to the fans. 'I know that you can travel to various parts of the European Community, four, five, six times cheaper than the costs that are being charged.

No wonder all this caused a fuss in the corridors of Britain's competition authorities.

The legacy, though, is felt most keenly by the supporters, denied the chance to follow their team abroad. The situation for some fans became so ridiculous that, in order to support their team, they had to make round trips of hundreds of miles.

Simon Mordue was studying in Germany when his team, Leeds United, was drawn against Stuttgart in the European Cup. He rang the club and told them of his situation. 'I explained that I was happy to tell them how I was going to travel, but their answer was quite simply no. If you want a ticket you have to fly back to Leeds, fly from Leeds to Stuttgart, then from Stuttgart to Leeds, and from Leeds to Germany.'

A dizzying and bizarre criss-cross journey across Europe for a fan who lived two miles from the ground. Simon told the club he would travel from his home and see the match independently, but he was told by Elland Road that there would be no tickets available.

'I sent off for tickets from Stuttgart and duly received three tickets in the post. I went down to Stuttgart the night before the match and there were hundreds and hundreds of Leeds fans who had bought tickets from Stuttgart.'

Fellow Leeds fan, Netherlands-based Guy Thornton, experienced similar problems: 'As far as trying to get official tickets, it's nigh on impossible unless you're willing to travel to Leeds and go on the Leeds trip – which, when you live in Amsterdam only an hour and a half from Eindhoven, involves a double trip costing £400 instead of £10.'

Leeds' response was to introduce extra pick-up points for all trips, but still it was not enough for Guy or his fellow european-based supporters.

Assistant Chief Constable Malcolm George of Greater Manchester Police looked after policing during Euro '96. He recognizes the anomalies in the way that clubs organize trips abroad, but says the first concern should be security. 'Security measures do seem to penalize the genuine fan, but any security means that a price has to be paid and the price is an element of restriction in movement.'

Such restrictive measures also mean that there will always

be people trying to find a way round the restrictions. Thus, fans who have complied with the club and travelled the expensive way with the official tours have often, to their fury, found themselves queuing at turnstiles next to fans who have made their way there independently.

They do this through small, independent firms run from small offices who take fans to games around Europe much more cheaply than the clubs.

Leeds' fan, Andy Peterson, travelled to Eindhoven with an independent travel agency in what turned out to be an unforgettable trip. 'When we started examining the tickets they were all for different parts of the ground and we thought this could be a bit dodgy. Then two police officers came up to us and asked if we were English, if we were going to the game, had we got tickets, and where were our passports?'

According to Andy, when they said their passports were in their rooms, things then started to get a little nasty.'Immediately I had my arms thrust behind my back and they said you are under arrest. I was cuffed with a piece of plastic and we were taken to a number of coaches which were obviously waiting for a large number of supporters. We were told that because we hadn't been carrying our passports, which I believe breaks some ancient Dutch by-law, we could be arrested.'

The Leeds fans were herded on to the coaches. 'They had miniature Police cells on board them which were probably about three-foot square and five-foot high. It was the worst thing I have ever gone through in my life, and I paid to go through it!'

They were clearly seen as hooligans, intent on causing trouble and they say they had been warned that there was a risk of arrest by the Dutch police. In their opinion, the firms don't want to tell them all the facts and risk losing money.

One hundred and twenty three Leeds fans were deported, their personal belongings, including passports, left stranded in Amsterdam. Despite the authorities on both sides of the North Sea having their details, they were classed as 'unofficial' supporters and 'unofficial' in the Netherlands meant thug.

It did not end there for those fans once they got off the ferry back home. In the Netherlands, Lex Heiss had already entered their details on to his database at the Dutch Centre for Information Football Vandalism in Utrecht. He refused to say how many Leeds fans were on the list, but all those arrested with Andy Peterson in Eindhoven were on it.

'All people,' he explains, 'who are arrested by a football match in the Netherlands are registered in our database. So a local police force, which arrests a person at a football match, will send the person's identity to us and we will put it in our database.'

It is understood that The National Criminal Intelligence Service (NCIS) in Britain also keeps the names of fans detained abroad on file, regardless of the apparent innocence of the alleged perpetrator.

Gwylem Boore and his brother Rhys were experienced travellers with the Welsh national team. In 1990 they went to Luxembourg for a European Championship qualifier. The brothers were on a train, which was stopped by police on the border. They were hauled off the train, their baggage was searched, they were photographed and then allowed to carry on with their journey.

Two years later they were following Wales again, this time to Belgium when there was a voluntary identity check. Gwylem and his brother chose to go through. 'I saw the police had a list and after I'd been let through the identity parade I walked around the back to look over the policeman's shoulder. I saw my name, my brother's name and a number of other people's names alongside the clubs they supported on the list. I was a bit concerned about this and my concern increased when my brother was taken to one side with somebody else and taken away to a Brussels police station.'

Gwylem claims that his brother was told he had been detained because his name was on a list of hooligans sent by authorities in England. Their mother, Anne, was given the same explanation when she made her own enquiries. 'If you listen to the duty officer at the British consulate, who was contacted by the Belgian police in response to a call from my eldest son, he was told that Rhys was detained because his name was on a list provided by the British police. If you read the documentation subsequently provided by the British consulate, they simply follow the later Belgian police line that Rhys had been drunk and disorderly. This could easily have been disproved if there ever was a trial because of the many witnesses willing to say what actually happened at the checkpoint.'

Letters sent to the Boores back up the name-on-the-list explanation and also confirm that the two men were placed on a police database after the train incident in 1990, when they were also supposed to have been involved in violent incidents. This, despite the fact that the violent incidents took part in a different part of the train.

All this leaves Rhys and Gwylem feeling, they say, very bitter.

'The idea of being innocent until proven guilty is reversed. You're guilty until you can prove you are innocent and even then that's not enough. We had to compile and amass a lot of evidence, send it off to various authorities, and say that what was being said was obviously not the truth, be it in regard to Luxembourg or Belgium. We have got witnesses, reliable people who can disprove the accusation which certain authorities have made and which has been accepted as fact.'

The Boores's case was taken on by Philip Leach, a legal officer with the civil rights group Liberty, who in turn contacted the European Commission. He demanded that the Boores's names should be taken off all lists. He feels the situation is totally unacceptable.

'The problem is that allegations are made and people, who do not have the opportunity to refute the allegations, are placed on lists. What should happen is that people should only be listed if there has been a criminal conviction. If this is not agreed, then people will not have the opportunity to have their say and will be treated as criminals.'

Philip Leach also handled the case of three Chelsea fans deported from Bruges. The implications, he says, are very serious.

'These actions by the authorities are serious and very fundamental breaches of people's human rights. To stop and search people, to photograph them and then to deport them involves violations of people's freedom of movement in Europe. The right to freedom of movement was established by the Treaty of Rome, and then supported more recently by the Maastricht Treaty. It is unlawful under European Union law for member states to deport people, unless there is a serious risk to public security – and that serious risk has to be caused by the individual concerned.'

The problem for the majority of peaceful fans is that they are tarred with the same brush as the minority who have blackened the name of English football for over twenty years.

Perry Ridley, another Chelsea fan, wanted to follow the club abroad and, after looking at the club package, chose to travel independently more cheaply and get his tickets from a Belgium friend.

'Myself and an Italian colleague travelled out there with ferry tickets etc., and there were about 200 Chelsea supporters on the ferry. We were all perfectly well behaved, but were met at the other end by the Belgian police. A policeman asked us why we were coming to Belgium. When we said for the football, he said I hope you've got a ticket. I said yes and showed it to him. By this time my Italian colleague had been allowed to go through. I showed him my ticket and he said it was forged. I said no way is that forged. He confronted me eye to eye and my mate said don't bother arguing – no one is going to get through. And everyone was turned away. All the police were looking at us as if we were scum. I was furious.'

So furious, in fact, he immediately wrote a letter to the Belgian ambassador to London. All he wants, he says, is an apology.

Two fans, same ticket, same destination, same purpose, but the British fan stopped while the Italian fan was allowed through. But that wasn't the worst of it. Perry Ridley had to deal with the possibility that his name was now on a list of potential football hooligans held across Europe and including the NCIS in Britain.

This apparent treatment of fans as second-class citizens was experienced by another Leeds fan, Stephen Davis, who travelled with a small, independent firm to Monaco. His nightmare began at Dover where he met the coach.

'There was banging on the windows at every check-point, *zeig heils* neo-Nazi type chants all the way through. This went on all the way down to Monaco. The driver put a pornographic film on the video. As soon as it was put on, a man said, look, you can't have this on I have a nine-year-old kid. The driver turned it off, but, after that, the bloke got abuse all the way through and was threatened at a service station as well.'

The small firms are quick to defend their tours and have banned the hooligan element concerned. They stress that they do all they can to keep the hooligans from travelling abroad.

The confusion that results from fans using 'official' and 'unofficial' tours means that segregation – a vital method of crowd-control – goes out of the window. Alan Roberts was the General Manger of Leeds United during the European Cup campaign. He says he understands fans wanting to see the team, but selling tickets to fans in the home-end is asking for trouble.

'What I can't condone is anybody knowingly selling tickets in the wrong area. All our fans know that a segregation policy exists; and that buying a ticket for the wrong end means risking not getting in and wasting their money.'

UEFA rules dictate that away-fans should be segregated, but the small firms have a simple way of getting hold of tickets, the just go directly to the European clubs to buy them – only though, after they have approached the clubs at home who almost inevitably turn their request down.

They say that there are still safeguards in place by the home club, and deny that they are behaving irresponsibly. Indeed, they make the assertion that some fans would not get to see the games without the existence of such firms and that others would still travel to matches, but with even less control. Rather than being attacked, they feel in fact that they should be commended for the service they provide.

Glyn Ford and his Brussels colleagues have answers to the

problem of segregation and to mistaking football fans for football hooligans. 'Rather than indicting a whole category of people, and making them second-class citizens, the solution seems to be that we should identify the perpetrators, give them the criminal records they deserve, and then stop them travelling on the basis of their records.'

Punish the thugs and give freedom to the fans. Simple, in theory. But the hooligan will always slip through the net. Malcolm George of Greater Manchester Police is convinced that the genuine fan needs more protection. 'It offends me that people can go to a game with no intention of being part of the game in the usual sense. They go to commit criminal acts of violence, and to manipulate situations so that they aren't actually putting the boot in, and can clear off as the trouble starts. Those people steer free of justice and that offends me as much as it does the genuine fan.'

A hooligan database like that of Lex Heiss in Holland is a dangerous method to combat hooliganism in Europe. In some respects, the English fan should be prepared to face the consequences in countries which have suffered, time after time, at the hands of followers at club and international level. But this means that the majority of innocent fans will have to go on paying for the sins of the few.

The clubs and FA, sick of having their names dragged through the mud, and mindful that another Heysel or Galatasaray may be around the corner, decided that some controls were needed. But these, in turn, caused more problems. Euro hit-lists, over-zealous policing and ticket policies falling foul of the competition authorities, all came about as direct consequences of the hooligans' reign of terror.

The solution, Glyn Ford feels, is not to restrict all football fans *en masse*, but 'to identify which football fans are uncontrollable hooligans'. One can't imagine another category of people, who are seen differently on different days of the week. Identify the people, convict them, then restrict their movement rather than everybody else's.'

Incidents at the World Cup show that the age of the organized hooligan is not dead, and that the onus is now on clubs and countries to make sure that fans like Gwylem and Rhys Boore are not penalized for life.

CHAPTER THIRTEEN

Heading for Injury Time?

The Link Between Football and Alzheimer's Disease

In April 1999, the former Celtic player Billy McPhail had his day in court. The 70-year-old Glaswegian was a sad and confused figure as he sat in among the austere finery of Scotland's legal best. Certainly, a far cry from the day in 1957 when he propelled himself into the green-and-white side of the city's pantheon of heroes by heading three goals past Rangers in Celtic's record 7-1 League Cup final victory.

McPhail has been suffering from the symptoms of pre-senile dementia for almost a decade. He and his family were convinced that in his 17-year career as a professional footballer, the frequent impacts caused by heading a heavy leather ball contributed to his degenerative mental illness. McPhail's lawyers were arguing that he should be entitled to a £70 a week disability payment under the terms of the industrial injuries act.

They are still arguing. Two courts have thrown the case out and it is now wending its way to the nation's supreme legal chamber, the Court of Session.

McPhail is not the first footballer to try and prove that the wear-and-tear of professional football has left him crippled and that his ailments, for the purposes of welfare benefits and compensation, should be classified as industrial injuries. There is a growing case-load of more than 60 former footballers with damaged knees, hips, and feet battling the point against a determined government. But his case highlighted a peculiar phenomenon; that of growing numbers of post-war footballers suffering from dementia in general and Alzheimer's disease in particular, whose doctors and lawyers were making the case that the illness had been triggered by years of heading footballs.

Some of football's most dramatic goals have come from headers and one of the iconic images of the English game in particular has been the strapping lad at the back repelling all comers with the flat of his forehead. The suggestion that hefty and frequent contact between a head and an object travelling at some lick would have a detrimental impact on that most sophisticated and delicate of organs, the brain, was never considered a serious proposition.

Irish international Johnny Carey was one of the game's greats. He captained Manchester United just after the war leading the 'Reds' to FA Cup glory in 1948 and following that triumph with the league title in 1952. United boss Matt Busby regarded him as a natural leader and forceful personality who could play in any position. Today Carey's widow, Margaret, lives quietly in a modern sheltered flat in leafy Cheshire. She likes to remember her husband when he was young and full of life.

'I used to go dancing with my friends on a Saturday evening at Chorlton Baths in Chorlton cum Hardy, so he danced with me and said, "Where shall we meet on Tuesday evening?" Just like that. I had never met him before, so I said you must be joking. Anyway I rather fancied him, so I did. I went out with him. He was only 19 at the time and was the nicest person you could wish to meet. I never heard him say anything nasty about anyone and it was the same when he got Alzheimer's. A lot of Alzheimer sufferers are difficult, he was not. He was so lovely all the time.'

It was in 1990 that Johnny Carey showed the first signs of the debilitating illness from which he would suffer for the rest of his life. 'He started to worry about silly things,' Margaret recalls, 'nothing to really worry about. Little things like driving the car. In fact, I had to stop him driving and that was the hardest thing I ever did.'

Soon Carey started to deteriorate even further. He took to wandering off in the middle of night and getting lost. On one occasion Margaret had to get the police to track him down. It soon became clear he could no longer stay at home and he was moved into a nursing home.

Carey died in 1995. But by then the death of an even more

famous figure with Alzheimer's, the former Manchester City and England manager Joe Mercer, had led a Liverpool GP to launch an investigation into the prevalence of the disease among footballers.

John Rowlands is a doctor at a family health centre at Maghull, a suburb of Liverpool. 'My main interest in a possible link between dementia and professional football started in the late 1980s when my friend Joe Mercer became ill. Then, just about the time Joe passed away, his wife Nora found herself going to the funerals of other famous footballers of the same age. And she discovered that more and more of them had suffered from dementia and possibly Alzheimer's disease. It was from that, that we began to wonder if there could be, in fact, a problem with this group of professional people.'

Geoff Twentyman is another friend of Dr Rowlands and a former player who is suffering from Alzheimer's. Twentyman, who played at Anfield in the fifties, wound up being chief scout for Liverpool when he retired as a player. He sits at home in a suburban Merseyside semi. He goes out for a walk most afternoons, not always finding his own way back. Physically he looks fine and is active, but it is clear he struggles to concentrate. 'I think it is the worst thing I have ever had in my life and I have had a lot of complaints, but this Alzinas...' His voice trails off.

Geoff's fading memories are preserved for his wife Pat in the neat, hand-written scouting log he kept on his travels. In it can be seen the initial notes on prospects over whom Geoff had cast his expert eyes years ago. Players like Phil Neal.

Phil Neal ... done well, good prospect, satisfactory game, worth a follow up.

Elsewhere in the book there are reports on John Toshack, Kevin Keegan, Ray Clemence – and even ones that got away like Francis Lee.

Pat recalls that when Geoff first started to suffer from Alzheimer's most people thought he had been hitting the bottle. 'A few people said they thought he was drinking too much, but he wasn't. It was just that he was confused.'

And that is the tragedy of Alzheimer's and other forms of dementia. Sufferers gradually descend into a twilight world of confusion.

'Time means nothing to Geoff, you know what I mean? He can get up at three am, and have a shower and a shave thinking it is time to get up. He will wake up in the middle of the night and ask "Who are you?" We have been married 46 years and he is asking me who I am.'

Dr Rowlands sent Geoff to see consultant neurologist Mark Doran at the Walton Centre in Liverpool, which specializes in head injuries, and attached a note asking if he had noticed a higher-than-average incidence of dementia in former footballers. Doran was intrigued. Together they drew up plans to track down as many former professional footballers as they could between the ages of 55 and 70, their plans given an impetus by news of the death of Bob Paisley, one of the most successful managers in English footballing history.

Paisley, who passed away in 1996, had succumbed to Alzheimer's at the beginning of the 1990s around the same time as Johnny Carey. But Bob Paisley, Joe Mercer and Johnny Carey were not the only famous footballers to die with the disease. Another was Spurs' great Danny Blanchflower and more recently the England manager Alf Ramsey. In fact, the Liverpool doctors tracked down around 35 footballers in their target range who had suffered from Alzheimer's or a similar condition. They also discovered they were not alone in their thoughts.

In 1989 tests on 69 players in Norway had discovered disturbances on their brain scans most likely due to neuronal damage caused by repeated minor head traumas. A couple of years later, the same Oslo scientists put 37 former Norwegian internationals through a battery of psychological tests. This time they discovered, '...mild-to-severe deficits of attention, concentration, memory and judgement in 81 per cent of the players. This may indicate some degree of permanent organic brain damage, probably the cumulative result of repeated traumas from heading the ball. We must conclude that blows to the head by heading show convincing evidence of brain damage similar to that found in patients who have sustained minor head injuries'.

Still more research, this time conducted in the United States in 1995, found that players who usually headed the ball ten times or more in a game had lower average IQs than team mates who headed the ball less frequently. They also did less well in tests assessing attention span, mental flexibility, facial recognition and visual searching.

More recently in 1997, Dutch neurologists focused on 53 professional footballers from a number of clubs in the Dutch league. They compared them to 27 élite athletes in non-contact sports. Both groups were subjected to a series of tests. The results showed players exhibited impaired performances in memory, planning and visual perception when compared to the non-contact sport performers.

According to the study, a player who takes part in 300 league games in a career will head the ball 2,000 times at speeds anywhere up to 100 miles an hour. The study concluded that, although heading the ball was a lot less traumatic than blows received by a boxer for example, the relationship between brain injury and heading the ball was a matter of public concern.

Under the rules of the game a football should weigh between 16 and 14 ounces. Although there has been much comment during recent World Cups about wayward shots being the result of a new lighter ball being used for international competition, this is a fallacy. The weight of a football before the game starts has always been between 14 and 16 ounces. What has changed has been the materials used to make the ball. Modern materials could conceivably cause less friction, meaning the ball will travel further for the same effort, but what is undoubtedly true is that the old leather ball absorbed water and got considerably heavier as the match progressed, anything up to 20 per cent heavier.

Still, even the waterproofed modern ball can pack some punch. The fastest shot recorded in the Premier League was by David Beckham in a match against Chelsea in 1997. It was tracked at 97.9 miles an hour. At the University of Manchester Institute of Science and Technology (UMIST) Professor Steve

Ried has created a test to measure the impact of leather on skull.

'What we decided to do was to see whether we could quantify the effect of the impact of a ball on the speed with which the head recoils on impact. There is a standard scientific index for this, believe it or not, called the Gadd Severity Index.'

The Gadd Severity Index is generally used to help develop safety features in cars and such like. An index reading of 1000 would cause severe concussion in a normal healthy adult. Professor Reid's test showed that had a head interrupted Beckham's shot it would have generated a reading of 300.

'The effect of any impact on the head is to generate shockwaves within the skull and within the brain. And these waves compress the brain. They compress the material and cause it to deform and then, when they have travelled through and reached a free surface at the back of the head, they are then reflected back causing tension within the brain.'

A glancing blow from a mistimed header could cause even more danger.

'It would complicate the problem because that would simply cause the head to rotate so that, instead of simply having compression and tension in the brain and between the brain and the skull, you could generate perhaps quite high-shear defamation there which might tear the ligaments and the connection between the brain and the skull causing a different kind of injury. Basically when you send stress waves through any material you deform them; and if you deform them rapidly and regularly you produce damage – and that damage can become permanent.'

By the mid 1990s the mounting evidence from Europe and the United States indicated the possibility of a problem, and it did not seem to matter whether people played with the old leather ball prone to becoming waterlogged or its modern equivalent. The Liverpool doctors planned a campaign called Neuro 96 coinciding with the Euro 96 football championship to raise a quarter of a million pounds for further research.

Mike Doran recalls, 'We have had promises of money, but nothing has materialized. To a degree, I am a bit surprised about this because I would have thought the research is in the interest of both the population at large and, more specifically, to those people who play football.'

Even when John Rowlands wrote to four Premiership clubs, asking for help, he got no joy. One club told him it was a matter for the Professional Footballers Association.

'I was a little bit surprised by that – the feeling that, without considering the cost, it should be the players themselves who needed to look into the research. So that was sort of the employees being told they have to look after their own health.'

Rowlands next port of call was the PFA. 'They were much more sympathetic and helpful, at least up to a point. They said they would support us with up to half the cost of the research but that we would have to go elsewhere for the rest. Unfortunately that proved very difficult. I contacted some drug companies but got no joy, and basically I am still looking.'

There was no Neuro 96. At the Professional Footballers Association HQ in Manchester, chairman Gordon Taylor has a bulging file of reports and correspondence relating to this topic. He says players feel the risk from heading the ball is so slight that in the past the PFA did not feel it worthwhile to stump up all the cash for a proper study, although the money is still on the table.

'We would be prepared to play a part in funding research to try to make it clear once and for all whether this is a fact or just a possibility. In an ideal world, it would be nice to know exactly what the consequences are of everything we do, so that we could all weigh up the risk.'

The truth is that establishing a definite link between heading a ball and Alzheimer's would not be welcome news to professional football. And whenever the matter is even hinted at in the press, football responds with maximum scorn. Take Bobby Gould's reaction to the report by the American study in 1995 that soccer players were more susceptible to brain damage than American football players.

'When you look at all the great headers of the ball back in the old days they aren't brain damaged, so it is hardly likely the players these days will be injured.'

That, as we know, is simply not true, but this comment was

followed up by the FA who issued a statement in the wake of the American research stating, 'There is no evidence that any player in this country has ever received head injuries from heading the ball'.

Heading the ball is undoubtedly an integral part of the game and for those who might want to ban it, it can be pointed out that people indulge in all sorts of sport – most obviously boxing – where the danger is considerably greater than anything generated in football. As Gordon Taylor puts it, 'It's a delicate problem' – delicate because if the clubs know about it but do not inform their players of the possibility they could lay themselves open to legal action.

There is another factor to take into account, this is the recent discovery of a gene which may help identify people at greater risk of dementia. Harry Cayton is the executive director of the Alzheimer Disease Society. 'Everyone inherits genes from their parents and there is a protein called Alipoprotein E, or Apo-E for short, which occurs in all human cells. We all have it but it occurs in three different forms, a bit like blood groups and if you have the Apo-E 4 gene, that appears to increase your risk of developing Alzheimer's later in life. If you carry the Apo-E 2 gene, that appears to inhibit the development of Alzheimer's. So the research suggests, for example, that if you have the Apo-E 4 gene, you are seven times more likely to develop Alzheimer's in later life than if you have the Apo-E 2.'

One in 25 people may have the Apo-E 4 gene. Peter Hamlyn, the London surgeon who saved the life of the boxer Michael Watson, says a simple genetic test would uncover those who may be at risk.

'With that information you could then give advice as to whether a career in contact sports was a sensible option, or at least inform people of the risk. I do not think you should go and screen a large number of professional sportsmen and tell them to give up. You can simply make the test available to young men and women who are in their teens and starting to develop an interest in contact sports. You might see clubs – before they take on juniors – screen them for this sort of thing. I would have thought that once parents know about this sort of thing, they will be very keen on it.'

The Football Association, now no longer so dismissive of the notion, has its own brain expert, the eminent neurologist Myles Gibson from Leeds. He feels that a survey of past footballers is of little use, but says there is probably a need to study current and aspirant professionals.

'We have studied the reports very carefully as they have come out and, although you can pick out scientific flaws in them from a scientific point of view, I have little doubt that this is something we have got to look at. But the difficulty is how to get the numbers right, how to get the correct aggregation of people so you can definitely say that, yes, footballers get Alzheimer's more commonly than the rest of the population.'

He does admit, however, that, in any other walk of life, he would not advise a young man to take up a job which requires him being repeatedly hit on the head for several months of the year. Like Harry Cayton he believes a profitable line of research would be to develop a test to screen for Apo-E 4.

'When you consider that just a few years ago we were not very knowledgeable about cardiac problems, but now we are in a position to test for heart problems and give very clear advice to youngsters, then the same may soon be the case in relation to the head.'

Should such a test become widely available – as seems likely in the none too distant future – then football clubs may well be forced to use it if they want their players to be insured. Football, in the past, has often behaved as if it were outside the law. The Bosman case was an excellent example of the game waking up to the fact that it is not. Likewise, as Duncan Ferguson discovered to his cost, a head- butt on the pitch, in the eyes of the law, is the same thing as a head-butt on a street corner. Thus proving a link between heading the ball and Alzheimer's could have massive legal implications.

Anthony Coombs is a Manchester solicitor who specializes in injury at work. 'It raises the possibility of future compensation claims by players against their clubs or possibly even the governing body which makes the rules. What you would have to show is that the club, or whoever, showed a lack of initiative in finding out something which in itself is not obvious. On this point a judge once ruled that "The employer must keep up to date but the court will be slow to blame him for not ploughing a lone furrow". It will depend a lot on the resources and wealth of the employer, but obviously football clubs are not poor.'

If this all sounds theoretical twaddle then consider the story of asbestos. At one time this was thought to be a harmless dust, but after it was discovered to be a killer. It was responsible for a series of worldwide insurance claims that led Lloyds of London and their 'names' to the brink of ruin in the late 1980s and early 1990s.

Much of the debate about Alzheimer's, needless to say, has passed the vast majority of professional footballers by. This means that players like recently retired Gary Mabutt, for example, live with a risk they know little or nothing about.

'I have spent most of my career as a centre-half and that, of course, is probably the position where you are heading the ball the most.'

Mabutt was concerned when he saw the evidence about the link between heading the ball and Alzheimer's, but is wary of over-reaction: 'Anything that can be detrimental to a professional footballer – or to anybody playing football – needs to be investigated, but basically players will consider that you get all sorts of injuries in football. We all know old footballers who have knackered knees or hips, but we are prepared to live with the risks because we love the game.'

There is no proven link between Alzheimer's and football, but then there has been precious little research into such a link, a point acknowledged by medical experts called by the Government opposing Billy McPhail's disability claim. What is clear is that there is an accumulation of anecdotal evidence, and evidence from small-scale scientific studies around the world, and that medical men involved with football no longer laugh at the suggestion that a key part of the game of football can cause brain damage.

The potential for legal action in the future means clubs and the game's governing bodies may not be as willing to live with the risks as most players undoubtedly would. The FA says that it is currently conducting an audit of injuries in the professional game. This is, it says, just the start of long-term research which will eventually help it to assess the effects that heading a ball has on the brain.

If it is found to be unacceptably dangerous, could it lead to headers being banned?

The FA's medical man, Myles Gibson, says it will certainly open a tortured debate. 'You can just imagine the sort of debate that would take place in the chambers of football if we come up with medical evidence that could force a change in the way in which football is played.'

Dr David Kernick, club doctor with Exeter City, has carried out a peer review of evidence so far and, like the FA's man, Myles Gibson, believes it is time for the footballing authorities to pull their finger out and pay for credible research.

He says, 'One of the problems with much of the research that has been carried out is that it has compared footballers with other sportsmen. Now, it is unfortunately true that many footballers do hit the bottle once they have retired and, as alcohol abuse is also a major trigger for dementia, it is possible that this rather than heading the ball has led to this seeming connection. Perhaps more definitive research could be obtained if, for example, goalkeepers were compared with central defenders.'

The immediate action for football should be to move quickly to discover if heading does trigger Alzheimer's in sufficient numbers to justify genuine concern. After all, we are talking about the biggest and richest sport in the world and such medical research as there has been, suggests that it is worth a serious look.

CHAPTER FOURTEEN

Customs and Exercise
The Players Who Use Soccer to Escape Persecution

The story of how a World Cup qualifier turned into something resembling a scene from a *Carry On* film will go down as one of the most bizarre in soccer history. But it also illustrates one of the most alarming developments in world sport over recent years – developments where international football has become a secret escape route from poverty, imprisonment and torture.

When the qualifying tournament for the 1994 World Cup started, Ethiopian hearts were full of optimism and hope. For a country that had dominated world headlines with famine and civil war, it was the ideal opportunity to garner good press and boost national pride. Their first game was away to Morocco and if they could return home with a draw then Ethiopia would be one step closer to reclaiming a position among the African football élite, a status it had not held for many years. But the cream of Ethiopian soccer talent had other plans. For them, playing away meant staying away, and they had no intention of ever coming back.

As there were no direct flights from Addis Ababa to the Moroccan capital Rabat, where the match was to be played, the squad of sixteen had to fly to Rome. The players were to spend the night there before flying on to Casablanca and then driving to Rabat.

The players had been given the night in a city boasting the unrivalled temptations of the Roman and Catholic empires. Thanks to the efforts of their country's ambassador in Rome, they were granted special visas which would allowed them to tour the likes of the Coliseum, the Vatican and the Trevi Fountain.

Some of the wide-eyed party, many of who had never been abroad before, decided when in Rome – roam. This was a horrible surprise for the assistant coach Getahun Wolbegiorgies who had no idea his squad was about to fall apart: `When we set out we had very good relations and very good attitudes in the team – I was not aware of any problem.'

When the coffee arrived for breakfast the following morning, there were empty seats at the table. 'After breakfast we were missing three players,' continued Mr Wolbegiorgies. 'We asked everybody where the players had gone, but no one seemed to know. We left for training in Rome with the remaining squad and the team manager went looking for the three who had disappeared.'

He did not find them.

Many international managers have experienced the situation where a few players have breached discipline on a night out abroad, but the trio of stop-out Ethiopians were not the sort to be found in the hotel room of a good-time Italian girl. Something more serious had happened. The police and the Ethiopian embassy were informed that three international footballers had gone AWOL in Rome. This was not an ideal start to a World Cup campaign, and things were about to get worse.

That afternoon as the team was about to catch its connecting flight to Morocco, there was another head count by the assistant manager. 'We had lost another three players, so, out of a squad of sixteen, we were now down to ten.'

It suddenly became clear to an increasingly desperate Mr Wolbegiorgies that the footballers were defecting. 'I couldn't believe it, because all the players had prepared so well for the game and we were expecting a good result.'

Mr Wolbegiorgies says his initial response was to phone home for advice: 'We telephoned from the airport and spoke to the President of the Ethiopian Football Federation (EFF). He told us to play the match with the remaining players. So we went to Morocco with eight outfield players and two goalkeepers. The remaining players were embarrassed about what had happened. The defectors had kept their plans a secret even from their own team mates. Everybody was shocked and sad.

The match was an incredible spectacle, having more in common with a Sunday league pub game than a World Cup qualifier. The Ethiopians kicked off with their reserve goalkeeper as an emergency centre-back and a 40-year-old deputy coach doing his best to keep up in midfield. The Moroccans were already favourites to win and, in front of a partisan – if bemused – home crowd, they set about ripping the makeshift visitors to shreds. It did not prove too difficult.

The score was four-nil by half time. The already shaky morale of the visitors had crumbled and two more Ethiopians chose to throw in the towel and sulk in the stands amid the confused Moroccan fans. No doubt their minds were as much on what had happened to their colleagues in Rome as on their colleagues on the pitch. The already under-strength side re-emerged for the second half further depleted with only nine men. At least the second goalkeeper and the ageing midfield coach were still fighting on like heroes.

For the next 20 minutes the remaining men scrapped valiantly, but predictably in vain. The middle-aged midfield stand-in was tiring and the goalkeeper was failing to handle his role as a centre back. When the game was a little more than a hour old the fifth goal went in. Three more Ethiopians immediately – and simultaneously – claimed to have suffered untreatable injuries and left the field. The two who had cried off at half time refused to return as substitutes. The Moroccan crowd, who had turned up to watch a serious World Cup Qualifier, found themselves witnessing a pantomime.

It was the turn of Algerian referee, Rachid Medjiba, to hold a roll-call. When he could only count six players on the Ethiopian side he had to abandon the game. FIFA rules dictate no team can play in any competition with fewer than seven players. The rule was developed to stop matches becoming farcical. In this case it was too late. After 65 minutes, the opening match of Group F of the African qualifying tournament for USA 94 was over. The spectators did not even get for a refund.

'The news was an embarrassment for both the Federation

and for the people,' said the Ethiopian Football Federation's secretary, Zerihun Biabegign, with endearing understatement as he sat in the offices of a proud federation that was one of the founding members of the Confédération Africaine de Football (CAF). 'Our people had expected a result from that match and they were embarrassed because the players ran away before the match.'

Assistant coach Wolbegiorgies said it wasn't just the officials who were red faced, 'Even the remaining players were embarrassed about the defecting players'.

The score stood at five-nil. FIFA considered, but rejected, the idea of throwing Ethiopia out of the World Cup. The country responded by committing itself to fulfilling all its qualifying fixtures. The selection net was cast wider around the Ethiopian league, and more players were drafted in.

Two weeks later, with six first-choice footballers still missing in Italy, they scraped a side together which earned a very creditable scoreless draw with Tunisia. But no matter how hard they fought in the remaining ties, the Rabat fiasco meant qualification for USA '94 was way out of reach. They even lost to West African minnows Benin.

And what happened to the half-a-dozen international footballers who jumped pitch to seek political asylum in Italy? Well, for a long period they were in hiding. It was assumed they had found somewhere safe and warm where the locals were willing to welcome six soccer internationals who did not speak Italian. Later, much later in fact, they were said to be working in factories near Rome and playing amateur soccer. No one is sure, certainly not Mr Biabegign: 'We have had no further contact with these players. It's very difficult. They fled. We don't know their whereabouts. If we knew their addresses we could contact them and pick them to play in the national team.'

But the runaways don't want to be found. The only motivation they had for an international cap was to get picked for an away-tie, and scarper.

To lose your international football team once is unfortunate, but to do it twice...

In the next five years the Ethiopians rebuilt their team from scratch. Their policy of developing young talent was rewarded when they won the East and Central African Youth Cup in 1995 and 1996. As the players matured, they were well placed to qualify for the finals of the 1997 African Nation's Cup – the continent's premier competition.

Again they were due to play Morocco away. The intervening period had failed to yield any direct flights to Rabat or Casablanca so, as before, the party flew via Italy. Once again, players deserted – not in dribs and drabs like the last time, but in a mass break out. Fourteen players, the doctor and the coach all disappeared into the Rome night.

When the manager, Mailissa Baihiro, arrived for breakfast, all he had for company was a goal keeper, one defender, four federation officials and a horrible feeling of *déjà vu*. 'When we woke up this morning they were gone,' he said at the time. 'We ran around but could not find them.'

Their beds had not been slept in, and their luggage had gone. This time there was no point in soldiering on to Morocco to face the further ridicule of Rabat fans. The loyal remnant returned home.

By the time Mr Baihiro landed in Addis Ababa, the 16 erstwhile members of his squad had come out of hiding. In the early hours of a January morning the lobby of a suburban Rome police station was filled with young men carrying kit bags. They were wearing Ethiopian Football Federation tracksuits and the pleading expressions of tired refugees. After spending a night sleeping rough on the streets, these international-quality footballers were seeking political asylum and had acquired a lawyer.

'For the first time they had passports and this made them feel truly free,' said Mario Lana concerning his newest clients. 'They met a compatriot who told them I was defending four Ethiopian hijackers.'

So, within hours of disappearing, they had formed an alliance with an Italian lawyer who was not only sympathetic to their aims, but had experience in representing Ethiopians who took unconventional advantage of air travel. He sounded ideal.

A year later most of these soccer stars were still in Italy, living in free accommodation provided by the Catholic church and gracing the factory floors of Arezzo, a small Umbrian town 160 miles north of Rome. A few had had trials with Perugia, in Serie A, but did not qualify for work permits – ironically because they had not played enough times for their country. They play a bit of amateur soccer, as do two of their colleagues who remained in Rome and now work as shop assistants.

These two great escapes are the most dramatic football defections to have hit Ethiopia, but they are not the only ones. Estimates of the number of international squad members who have leaked from Ethiopian away-trips range from 80 to 110. Federation Secretary Zerihun Biabegign is left picking up the pieces: 'We have lost over 100 very talented players over the last 25 years which means that the standard of football will drop. That should not continue.'

It has already continued for too long. Ethiopia, once the most powerful of Africa's footballing lions, has been reduced to a minor role in the pride. Nations like Cameroon, Nigeria and Ghana were only cubs when Ethiopia was king, now the roles have been reversed, largely because defection disease has taken the best players of every Ethiopian generation.

The first African Nations Cup was held in Sudan in 1957. The founding nations were Sudan, Egypt, South Africa and Ethiopia. Of those it was the Ethiopians who brought the most mature soccer heritage to the party. Addis Ababa did not suffer five years of occupation by the fascist Italians from 1936-41 without picking up a little soccer, and teams with Italian names like Consolata and Piazza Roma were dominating the local scene.

As football spread through the continent, Ethiopia remained at the centre of events. The EFF provided CAF with its longest serving president, Ydnekatchew Tessema, who oversaw the growth of soccer in Africa for 15 years. Ethiopia also had success on the pitch. In 1962 the third African Nations Cup was held in Addis Ababa and won by the hosts. The organization of the event was to fall to the EFF twice more. But it was around the time of their third hosting, in 1976, that the defection trend got into full swing.

Six players from Mechal, the Ethiopian army club, went missing. They reappeared in Egypt seeking political asylum. It was to be a habit that would develop and grow – persistently robbing the nation of its dominance and pride.

One of the players from the second aborted Morocco match explained why the defections continue: 'It is better to be in a free nation where one can move freely, rather than live in a climate of oppression,' he said while waiting to be seen by an immigration official in Rome.

Oppression was certainly not the motivation for the defection of soccer soldiers in 1976, and it is hard to justify such a claim for many of the rest. One explanation has to be money. The EFF is run on amateur lines with players receiving what amounts to pocket money. When players find out how the other half lives, the temptation becomes clear.

The Ethiopian government insists that all people have freedom of movement, but the footballers tell a different story. They say that it is practically impossible to get a passport unless you are a government official or an international sports star.

The majority of the Ethiopian defectors are from the Amara tribe who, until 1991, provided the country's government. The human rights record of their reign was appalling with reports of random imprisonment, torture and murder. When a civil war brought power to a different tribe, the ordinary Amara people suffered the revenge that was due to their brutal leaders. 'Amnesty International has published a report into human rights abuses in Ethiopia since 1991,' states Amnesty researcher Alistair Fearnie. 'We have been concerned with cases where the Amara people have been detained because of their non-violent political beliefs.'

Amnesty's report claims that in the first two years after the overthrow of the Amara government 20,000 people were imprisoned for their opposition to the new government. The document credits – if credit for such things can ever be given – the security forces with inventing a new form of torture. Arms are tied together tightly with plastic strips, cutting off the blood supply. After hours of excruciating pain, paralysis of the lower arms sets in.

Football's authorities are not keen to admit that their sport is used as a vehicle for political defection, but Mr Fearnie knows it is. 'The reality for most Africans is that they do not have the resources to go overseas. Sports people obviously do have that opportunity to leave and that puts them in a more fortunate position. From Amnesty's point of view that shouldn't be relevant. If it's true that they will be tortured and persecuted when they are sent home, then they should be granted asylum regardless of whether they are international sports stars.'

Of course it is not just football that attracts the hopes and dreams of those desperate to escape. The lives of Amara people seem so hopeless that even terrified young girls cling on to sporting ambition with the hope of defecting.

It was a bitterly cold morning in the north east of England when, just before dawn, four slim, young black women flagged down a taxi. The driver laughed when they gave him a hesitant one-word instruction: 'London'. He drove them to Durham railway station where they spent all their money on four single tickets.

Two days earlier one of these women had helped the Ethiopian team win gold in the junior race of the 1995 World Cross Country Championships. Now, at 17 years old, she had decided to follow the example set by her footballing compatriots. With the world of athletics poised to offer her a glorious future, she focused on the only goal she had ever had – freedom.

'We just wanted to get to London because we knew there were many Ethiopians in London,' recalled Birhan Dagne and her three fellow runaways; two other athletes and a coach. 'We couldn't ask for asylum where we were because we couldn't speak any English.'

The quartet were in Durham for an event in which Ethiopia had a proven record of success. Their government, though, was starting to wise up to the sport-for-passport movement. Teams competing abroad were still given passports, but now they got security guards as well. The squad of runners in Durham were housed in student accommodation. The university campus had a fence around it, and the runners were watched through the day by government staff. The guards were supposed to be for the protection of the athletes, but Birhan and her friends knew the truth. The four runners felt like prisoners.

Terrified and freezing cold, the four young women jumped over the Durham University fence at five o'clock in the morning under the cover of frost-filled darkness. Their daring plan had been hatched long before, but, says Dange, they had told no one:.'We couldn't trust anyone. Ethnic groups were split up by the security people so that we couldn't talk without somebody else hearing and telling the security people. We were really frightened. If any of the Federation knew we were running out, then we would have been in real trouble. All we wanted was to get out of that place. We didn't care where we were going, we just escaped.'

Birhan said she knew of people from home who had been imprisoned by the government. She feared torture if she returned. 'If they make us return to Ethiopia we would rather commit suicide than go back. Now that we have tried to be free, we would be tortured in Ethiopia.'

Birhan's story has a happier ending than the factory-working footballers. She was allowed to stay in Britain, married and moved to Bethnal Green. When the World Cross Country Championships came to Belfast in March 1999 she wore a Great Britain vest and competed against the new wave of Ethiopian runners. As a member of Essex ladies she has shot to the top of British rankings. She is still young enough to go on and win medals for her new country.

The runaway runners were right about at least one thing – there are a lot Ethiopians in London. There is a complete football league of them. On artificial pitches, 20 feet below the M4 fly-over in Labroke Grove, teams with names like *Tendros* and *Yednekachew-Teseme* compete every weekend. Most of the players are refugees. Many of them have come to England via the well-worn routes of business and tourism, but some are runaway internationals. They shy away from interviews. It is unclear if they fear detection by Ethiopian security officials or UK immigration officers.

One of the referees in this league is Getachew Amsalu, a man with 14 years experience in leagues in both Addis Ababa and London. Every week he adjudicates on matches between players he knows deserve a better standard of competition than West London provides: 'They are good players, trying to get bigger clubs, but until that time they play in this league'. The referee understands that travel is the main reward for top players. 'Yes, they are trying to get some means to be free, otherwise everything is blocked for them. It saddens me that the best players are leaving Ethiopia, but they have no chance to travel unless they are sportsmen.'

Seyoun Samuel plays for one of the West London teams. He was a tennis international when he defected. 'Once you are selected for the national team, everything becomes easy. After people saw that players in the national teams could get passports without hassle, a new motto developed – *"Sport for Passport"*.' Like most players, he used the door only once. He has no intention of going back.

All over the world, sport-for-passport is causing problems. And you do not even need to be a real sportsperson to try it.

When the twelfth Asian Games were held in Hiroshima in 1994 an ambitious, if a little over optimistic, bunch of Filipinos tried to hijack the sport-for-passport bandwagon. A bus arrived on a ferry to Japan with 54 passengers. They claimed to be the Philippine volleyball team. Immigration officials became suspicious when they noticed that all the party were under 5ft 7in tall. Doubts grew when a search of the bus failed to uncover any sports equipment. Checks were made and one crucial fact was discovered. The Philippines had not entered a volleyball team. The bus was turned around and 54 desperately disappointed bogus sportsmen were sent home.

The list of defectors in Hiroshima did not suffer too much from the missing Philippine contingent. This was the biggest Asian games ever and of the 7,000 real sportsmen and women there were plenty of potential escapees. A daily disappearance register kept the reporters busy. Harry Peart was covering the games for the BBC World Service. He says the press box was like a missing persons' bureau: 'They ranged from Sri Lankans, Nepalese a Bangladeshi and some Iranians. They just disappeared, it became a daily occurrence'. These defectors were not looking for asylum like the Ethiopian footballers had been. The motivation was simple – they had a yen for the Japanese currency and were willing to work anywhere. Harry Peart says there were stories of visiting squads being approached even before travel with the tempting offer of a career in the Japanese black economy. 'People were recruited for what they called the 3D jobs – difficult, dirty or dangerous,' claims Peart.

Even now there are people toiling at the grimy end of the Japanese industrial underworld whose principal qualification is that they were one of the top athletes in a small Asian country in the mid-1980s. They have traded the prospect of a gold medal for the certainty of a silver dollar.

Equally, if anyone can be bothered to search the lower end of the Swedish economy they will probably find top Nigerian footballers.

In 1993 the Ugbowo Bombers under-18s side took part in the Gothia Cup – Sweden's biggest ever youth championships. The players attracted rave reviews for their entertaining football, but once the event was over they grabbed even bigger headlines as 'the lost soccer team' last seen leaving a hotel in Stockholm.

Four years later, two more Nigerians travelled to Sweden for trials with Helsingborgs on the south west coast. When they failed to secure contracts with the first-division side they vanished.

The Swedish authorities had had enough. In 1997 they refused entry visas to a team of 13-year-olds from Nigeria. Despite their age the teenagers were deemed likely to seek asylum, and turned away.

Not all countries share Sweden's reluctance to be the destination for sporting defectors. Nations with an eye to political point-scoring can positively encourage what we might call the 'vanishing player' syndrome.

In terms of medals per head of population, there is no more successful Olympic nation in the world than Cuba. Castro's revolutionary government insists on amateurism, even for the cream of Cuban competitors, so the financial incentive for defection is great. What is more, every time a Cuban team travels abroad there is an army of American anti-Castro zealots with the sole purpose of tempting possible defectors to become runaways.

Every day of the Central American Games in Peurto Rico in 1993, a plane flew over the top of the stadium. Trailing behind the plane was a banner giving out a phone number for the Cuban team to ring if they wanted out. Billboards encouraged the Cubans to listen to the radio, especially a station called The Voice of the Cuban American National Foundation. Between the records of Salsa and Mambo music, sportsmen and women who earn less then ten pounds a month are lured towards capitalism with the prospect of untold wealth. Thirty-four athletes succumbed. They became the latest members of an army of hundreds of Cuban sporting defectors.

One unconfirmed story involved an un-named Cuban pole vaulter who flew to Spain for a junior competition. When the plane landed he calmly walked down the steps. As his feet touched the runway he began to run away. Leaving luggage and friends he sped passed dazed airport security guards and headed straight for the perimeter fence. With one gigantic leap he was free, and never seen again. It is thought he had a welcome party arranged and a new life to begin.

True or not, it is tales of heroism like this that fuel the sport-for- passport phenomenon. It's a political act. The anti-Castro campaigners know that every defector is a blow to communism, just as every loyal medal winner puts a satisfied smile behind Castro's beard.

Sport, and especially football, is of great importance to world order. Countries, particularly those who lack economic clout, can derive immeasurable good press on the back of a sporting success. Just as league status can bring image and status to a small town in Britain, a place in the World Cup finals bestows importance on an otherwise undistinguished nation.

Would Brazil really have the respect it enjoys if it was not for the fact that the country can play great football?

For this reason sport-for-passport will continue to be a problem. While Ethiopia is getting bad press for famine and war, it needs the good publicity of a competitive football team abroad. However, because there is famine and war, and apparently restrictions on international travel, the very players the government relies upon to be sporting ambassadors are tempted to defect. For them, international football is just a means to an end, and their lives are so poor that the prospect of a job on an Italian factory floor is an end worth achieving.

Nigeria's footballers did their government a huge favour when they won Olympic gold medal in Atlanta and when they reached the second round of France 98. The nation did not look so great on either of the occasions when players disappeared in Sweden.

Football's governing bodies – either the world body FIFA or UEFA in Europe or CAF in Africa – are caught in the middle of sport-for-passport. Their member nations who suffer from defection disease want security tightened up to avoid the bad publicity. But can a sports body risk the accusation of turning training camps into prison camps and turning players into prisoners? So long as some nations deny travel to their subjects, either by refusing visas or because of poverty, football will be used as a route to political asylum.

Ethiopia has changed its approach to football and flying to try to stop the rot. A small number of players are now based overseas while still representing their country. Dahir Mohammed, who went to the USA in 1998 to join major league team the New England Revolution, is the best example. The EFF's theory is that it is better to allow the talent to drain abroad and keep in touch, rather than to risk further disappearing acts.

Direct flights from Addis Ababa to Rabat might be a good idea as well.

CHAPTER FIFTEEN

Mind Games
English Football's Rejection of Sports Psychology

In 1996 the pressure really got to Kevin Keegan. As Margaret Thatcher might have advised him, `This was no time to go wobbly,' but he did. And he did it in front of watching millions during the run-in to the Premier League title race that year.

'I would love it, really love it, if we beat them,' spluttered Kevin of an up-and-coming match with Leeds United. The Sky football anchor man, so bemused by Keegan's intensity of emotion, did not really know what to say next. An uncomfortable silence followed. It was painful to watch.

The cause of the erstwhile Newcastle United manager's ire had been Alex Ferguson's contention, after a hard-fought draw with Leeds, that the Yorkshire club would go easy on title rivals Newcastle when they played them, inferring that should the title find its way to Tyneside, the achievement would be a lesser one because everyone reserves their best effort for playing Manchester United.

It probably was not a conscious psychological dig on Alex Ferguson's part but it is often held up in the press as an example of his cunning use of psychology. It was, however, certainly the defining moment in Keegan's reign at St James's Park. Newcastle's charge for the championship subsequently stalled and was never as convincing under his management again.

Ferguson follows in a long line of managers like Brian Clough, Matt Busby or Bill Shankly who similarly have been lionized not only as masters of motivation but also as supremos at 'psyching out' the opposition. The cult of such managers has contributed to a central conceit in British football that they can do without experts. Certainly when it comes to matters of the mind, the message is football can look after itself.

Indeed of all the experts who hold qualifications recognized and respected elsewhere in the world of sport, none attracts as much scorn within footballing circles in the UK as a sports psychologist. One of the few sports psychologists in the UK who has worked on long-term contracts at football clubs is Dr Richard Cox of the University of Edinburgh.

'When I was first engaged, the manager said to me I believe in what you can offer my players, but whatever you do please keep it quiet that you are working here. I asked him why? He replied because I do not want to become a laughing stock in Scottish Football.'

The consequence of such thinking is that a coaching tool, highly valued elsewhere in the world (including at many Continental clubs) has been denied to the vast majority of the players plying their trade on these shores. Goading the opposition, or even your own players, is seen as the only psychology a manger or player will ever need.

For Dr John Masters of the University of Stirling, such baiting is as likely to achieve the opposite of the intended effect, 'Spending time trying to influence your opponent's state of mind is diversionary, at the very least. You can have no idea what effect your comments will have. You may induce anger, but will that diminish your opponent's performance? It might make them more determined.'

Despite the overwhelmingly negative attitude towards sports psychology within football there have been a few managers brave enough to live with the prospect of being a laughing stock among their peers. The first of this still very select band was Keith Burkinshaw who managed Tottenham way back in 1980. Ironically this team included Glenn Hoddle who, arguably – having elevated Eileen Drewery as healer-cum-counsellor to the England team – has made it more difficult for sports psychology to operate in football.

Burkinshaw had already displayed a flair for the unorthodox by bringing Argentina's World Cup stars Ossie Ardiles and Ricky Villa to White Hart Lane in the wake of the 1978 World

Cup at a time when foreigners were considered exotic but risky investments in the British game. By 1980 he was in the final stages of building a team that would go on to lift two FA Cups and a UEFA Cup in four seasons.

However, he was conscious that, even in the best Tottenham teams, there was a soft centre, and he wanted to introduce a bit of steel into his side. 'When you have been in football for some time, you realize that mind is a big factor.'

Burkinshaw invited a London-based consultancy, run by John Sire and Chris Connolly, to work with the squad. Inevitably word got out, and he recalls that 'good fun was had by all on the back pages of the tabloids. The *Daily Mirror,* I think, had a picture of a black couch right across the back page and another newspaper had a banner headline that read "White Coats at White Hart Lane". This was the perception – that psychiatrists there to treat people who had problems.'

Happily, Keith Burkinshaw knew his psychiatry, the treatment of mental disorder, from his psychology, the knowledge of how the mind works. 'Sports psychology is about helping people to improve their performance and be better than their opponents, and to develop all aspects of their game, both mental and technical. So it is made up of doing exercises which happen to be mental rather than physical.'

Sire and Connolly worked as part of the coaching staff at Spurs for five years, which included the years when Hoddle, Ardiles and company carried off the three cups. He struggled for a moment to place Sire, 'To be honest, most of us treated it pretty lightly. Certainly some of the senior players who had been round the block a bit took little or no notice at all. There was a lot of sniggering behind his back.'

Sire, not surprisingly, is more positive, 'Keith Burkinshaw believes that we made a tangible difference to the team and helped them during that period when they were very successful'.

Whichever way you look at it Burkinshaw's move was at least brave in the context of how it was likely to be greeted by his peers, 'How much you are getting from it, is not something that you can divine exactly. But I did feel it was helping us.'

The late 1980s were something of a dark age for English football. It was a time when our clubs seemed to lose the plot after a decade or two of European dominance. Many point to the post-Heysel ban as being the root cause of English football going backwards during this period.

But it was not only on the pitch that our European rivals were stealing a march. There was much activity off the pitch, with improved coaching, new ideas on fitness and diet and, yes, even psychology being integrated into the foreign game. It cannot be argued that the lack of sports psychology was the root cause of our football decline relative to Italian, Spanish or French football during those years, but the derision that is heaped on the notion of psychologists in football shows how resistance to new ideas in general has handicapped the development of the game here.

FA Technical Director Howard Wilkinson is certainly a fan of sports psychology, but he recognizes that it is not something you can impose on players who by and large are a conservative bunch, 'You cannot force it. Players have to come to the table appreciating the value of the proposition'.

In other words, it needs to be sold – not easy at English clubs where many managers would see a psychologist more as a threat than an asset. After all, when, increasingly, the Chief Executive is the man with the ultimate say on buying and selling, and the first-team coach is the man with day-to-day contact with players on the training field, what is there left for a manager to do but pick the team and motivate it?

Like Spurs, Bolton Wanderers have the reputation of being a bit of a soft touch. They have yo-yoed between Premier and first division in the past few years. Anyone with a passing interest in the club will know that their fate has been sealed not by regular thrashings from all comers, but more often than not by drawing too many games which they really ought to have won.

But suggest a sports psychologist to Colin Todd (the man who guided them through this purgatory) and he positively bristles, 'I do not see that there is any need for one of those. Managers and coaching staff know the breed of the player and know what makes them tick. Players are only human and if you have an indifferent spell, you look back at certain things with them and all of a sudden it will come right. But psychology – that's not for me.'

Just before you get the idea that Colin Todd is an exception in his reaction to the idea of psychology as a coaching tool, he is not. Of the top 44 clubs surveyed by *On The Line* in 1997, three quarters of them told us they had never used the services of a sports psychologist, nor would they consider doing so.

Here are some of the replies: 'The coaching staff and manager are all ex-players. We know how to deal with players and get the best out of them.' 'We have sought outside help for players with personal problems, but on the football side all that stuff is dealt with by the managers and coaches.' 'We are all ex-footballers on the coaching side and we think we know how to gee the lads up.'

So, the philosophy which has dominated the English game for generations – that only former footballers know what is good for current ones – is still prevalent. When even the wisdom of employing a fully-qualified physiotherapist struggles for universal acceptance, what chance has psychology?

At the vast majority of clubs, the answer is not a lot. Most managers remain hostile or at least sceptical towards the notion. But not Jim Smith of Derby County. 'Within certain scientific bounds, I am pretty open-minded about anything that will improve a team and the players.'

Jim Smith is the longest serving manager in England. He certainly has the look of a traditional 'Boss', but is anything but. Psychology is a key part of the coaching process at Derby County and the east Midlands club is unique in the football leagues as the only club which employs a full-time sports psychologist. His name is Bill Beswick.

'When I first came here, there was no doubt that the players thought that coming to see "Psycho Bill", which is what they called me, was a sign of weakness. There is also no doubt now that players enjoy seeing me, enjoy talking through their problems.'

Jim Smith is likewise pleased with the work that Bill has

done. 'His common sense approach clicked with me, and he certainly played his part in ensuring that certain individuals were outstanding. They have done more in the Premier League than I ever thought they would. A lot of that is down to Bill Beswick.'

John Sire says that Derby County appears to appreciate what sports psychology can and cannot do for its team and, more importantly, understands that it is not a miracle cure. 'The key thing to get across is we are not part of the medical set up, we are part of the coaching staff. Our first job is to sit down with the coaching staff and manager and say how would you like this team to be? Then we help the team discover qualities within itself.'

Much-travelled striker Ashley Ward was at Derby when Bill Beswick first arrived. 'I had quite a few troubles with injuries and things and, in those circumstances, it is easy for your head to drop and for you to get a bit depressed. But when you chat to Bill he puts things in perspective. The majority of the players have found it very helpful for the game.'

Bill Beswick helped Jim Smith slaughter one of football's greatest sacred cows – 'take each game as it comes'. Under Bill's guidance Derby now thinks more long-term, dividing the season into blocks and setting points targets for each sequence.

Says Bill, 'There are times in the season when we play clubs that we get points from and we will be riding high and life will be good. There are times in a season when we hit fixtures that we are really not going to get that much from. If you know that and predict ahead and focus on a certain period that is likely to bring you a dip in points, you do not necessarily lose self-belief. If you present the likely course of season to players in those terms, it helps them get off the hook. And, of course, if a result goes against the grain, like when we beat Manchester United 3-2 at Old Trafford, it has a lasting impact on morale.'

Sports psychology was not an entirely new concept to Jim Smith. In 1989 when he was managing Queens Park Rangers he allowed a psychologist in to work with the team. As it happened, it was John Sire and the whole experiment was filmed for the

BBC 1 science programme *QED*. It can hardly be claimed that the programme did psychology any favours. When Sire walked through the door QPR were top of the table, when he left they were third. Despite this, Smith like Keith Burkinshaw, saw some value in the experiment and decided to handle it differently at Derby.

'I changed the rules a little bit. I did not want any group psychology. I wanted one-to-one because it is a personal thing and the individual has to see some value in it and want to do it. When you get a group, sometimes they all mess about.'

This was certainly evident in the *QED* film which included numerous scenes of Sire earnestly lecturing while rows of footballers smirked. At Derby, Smith made sports psychology voluntary. If players wanted to use Bill Beswick's services, they could – and it appears they did.

'We have found that, slowly but surely, nearly every individual has spoken to Bill at one time or another. I think in all honesty a lot of the stuff that Bill does, a manager might do without knowing it. But we do not have the time to work with each individual, to work problems out, and spend an hour or so speaking with them. But when that is your profession, then you do have the time.'

Smith's attitude to sport psychology is almost text-book according Dr David Collins, who is chairman of the Sports Psychologists group at the British Association of Sport and Exercise Science (BASES). 'It takes a lot longer than people believe. On a couple of occasions I – and my some of my colleagues – have been approached in the following way: "We have our cup final in a couple of weeks, can you come in and work with us?"'

Unfortunately for the credibility of sports psychology this short-term input approach has often been the role into which it has been cast.

Graham Taylor sprung a psychologist on the England team on their ill-fated trips to Poland and Norway in 1993. Less famously, Bradford hired a sports psychologist a day before its promotion play-off clash with Blackpool in 1997. They lost 2-0, dumped the psychologist and won the second leg 3-0.

Such anecdotal tales tend to stick in footballers' minds and, as a result, whenever psychologists walk through the gates many say to themselves, 'Now we *really* are in trouble'. Sports psychology has tended to be associated with last throw of the dice when everything around a club is going pear-shape.

There is also an overriding impression that psychologists are there to fix something that is broken. Not so, says Steve Bull, who is sports psychologist to the England cricket team.

'If a player has personal problems, or is suffering from stress or depression I do not see it as my job to start tinkering. I would refer him immediately to a clinical psychologist. They know how to deal with those problems. My role is to try and enhance the mental capacity of the players solely in relation to their game.'

So a team psychologist is not there to help sort out the Stan Collymores or Paul Gascoignes of this world (although of course he or she could help). Rather the aim is more to get the best out of Alan Shearer, Michael Owen or David Beckham. This is a remarkably difficult message to get across in English football, where that headline about the white coats at White Hart Lane, still resonates strongly through the game.

Other sports have no such problems. Psychologists, for example, have been widely used in cricket, rugby, athletics, tennis, golf, etc., for many years. One of Dr Collins's customers is Karl Grant, a Great Britain weight lifter.

'It does not feel like therapy. It feels like an important part of coaching. To me, it is what coaching is all about. I do not need someone to go "Come on, lift". I can do that for myself. What I need is someone to help me focus. That is what Dave Collins does for me and it is what I need.'

Paul Lawrie, the 1999 Golf Open winner, had worked with Dr Richard Cox for a year prior to the Carnoustie event which he won so famously after a tense play-off.

There is another reason, apart from its innate conservatism, that football continues to rebuff the advantages that sports psychologists have to offer, and that is – as the world's most popular and richest sport – it is also open season for every crank and quack with the gall to enter the market.

Howard Wilkinson, a fan of sports psychology in football, who used psychologists while manager at both Sheffield Wednesday and Leeds, says, 'I was offered the prospect of miracle transformations on an almost daily basis – and I know other managers were, too. Certainly in my years at Leeds, I lost count of the number of different disciplines that approached me making all sorts of claims about what they could do for us'.

Given this, it is not surprising that the majority of managers file such approaches under 'Bonkers'. But for the minority who would like to take matters further there is the problem of sorting the wheat from the chaff. In the end, managers like Alan Smith, ex-Crystal Palace and Wycombe, ended up taking a shot in the dark. 'I did not have anyone to turn to. I did not know who to go to. Quite often I was talking to people on the back of a phone call or because I had read about someone.'

At another club I spoke to, a very plausible sounding psychologist was hired and ended up trying to interfere in team selection, training techniques, tactics, and practically every other aspect of the club. In the end, he was escorted from the training field and barred from the club.

Despite the existence of such examples, Alan Smith still believes that psychology has much to offer football clubs, 'When I was first appointed manager at Crystal Palace, the club had just been relegated and I thought we needed someone to lift both the players and me. In the first year we won the championship and we did employ two or three psychologists. Despite varied experiences, I still believe sports psychology can be a real help to a team'.

So does Bobby Gould, the much-travelled football club manager and erstwhile manager of Wales. Inspired by the work Steve Black has done with the Welsh rugby union squad, Gould invited sports psychologist Ian Cockerill to work with the Welsh football team at the start of the European Championship campaign.

Gould says, 'I am into this in big way. If a sports

psychologist can give any Welsh player an extra five per cent to his game, then it has to be a good thing. These people are specialists in their own field. They know what they are talking about, what to say, and how to give players that extra buzz.'

Certainly Wales buzzed with uncharacteristic confidence when it went to Copenhagen and beat Denmark in the opening match of the campaign. But it was all downhill from there and Gould himself threw in the towel after a gutless display which saw his team thrashed 6-0 by Italy.

But there was a key difference between the Welsh football and rugby team and their application of sports psychology. Steve Black has been given a decent run with players who, when they are not representing their country, are playing rugby in Wales. He has had the opportunity to work with the squad all year round because they are on his doorstep. This is not true of the Welsh footballers who are spread all over England and only work with a psychologist piecemeal. Black has also had the whole-hearted support of not only team manager, the Kiwi Graham Henry, but also the Welsh Rugby Football Union who are happy to pay his wages.

The FA of Wales, however, blocked Gould's request for a full-time post for a sports psychologist within the organization. It decided that 'this was not the way forward for the national side'.

Perhaps this decision needs to be considered in the light of possible public reaction to such a move, given the Eileen Drewery fall-out under Glenn Hoddle, and Kevin Keegan's decision to hire a folk singer-cum-comedy script writer to gee up the England team before it faced Poland in a European qualifier.

Sports psychologists are unsure exactly what effect Drewery has had on their stock in the football world. Dr Richard Cox, who says that at the very least it put the matter of mind on the agenda, also accepts that for some people it only served to reinforce ideas that mental coaching has no part to play in the game. In common with his peers, Dr Cox also cites the cult of the manager as being the biggest stumbling block to the acceptance of sports psychology.

'Very few managers understand the concept of motivation. You have those who bawl and shout at players, seemingly oblivious that more often than not this is counter-productive. I was shocked when I went to work at clubs to find that players rarely have any idea of how their colleagues see them or what their value to the team is. No one bothers to tell them. Incredible.'

Interestingly, this point was picked out by Alex Ferguson when he gave an interview to the German football magazine *Kicker*, a month after he had lifted the European Champions Cup. 'When I started coaching, my main job was to improve my players' shape, balance my team and get them to play football... Nowadays you have to coach their minds – teach them about preparation. These players must recognize each other's qualities and appreciate the talents of those around them. I always tell the players we need at least eight of them to play well if we are going to have any chance of winning.'

If Manchester United has employed a sports psychologist, it is not something it shouted about. Clearly, Sir Alex Ferguson is a talented leader, some people are, but that does not negate the need for qualified mental coaches at football clubs. Certainly Manchester United's first – team coach, Steve McClaren, is a fan of sports psychology. He spent three years at Derby County, where Bill Beswick was on the staff, before being snapped up by Manchester United.

A typical case of football sticking by football and living unquestioningly with its past, is the number of clubs that persist with a bonus-payment system. Dr Cox has bad news on this front, 'I recently conducted a study of 52 Scottish club players to try and discern what motivational impact bonus payments had. Almost unanimously the result was none at all. I carried this further and a team was put on higher payments to win a match with no discernible increase in motivation. The next week it was offered a day off training instead which produced a transformed performance'.

As football in this country inches towards a more holistic approach of player preparation, psychology – while making some inroads – is still at the back of the queue behind sports science, sports medicine, nutrition and fitness training. Even if particular managers decide to use sports psychologists, you can bet that the clubs concerned will not be terribly up-front about it.

Increasingly, however, individual players are visiting sports psychologists. The problem for them is much the same as that faced Alan Smith at Crystal Palace – sorting out the charlatan from the real thing. Only 15 practising sports psychologists are accredited by the British Psychological Society (BPS), then there is the British Association of Sport and Exercise Science (BASES) which has a further 65 members, so properly trained sports psychologists are thin on the ground.

You might have thought that the FA or the Premier League, if they took player preparation as seriously as our rivals do, might have come across an organization such as BASES and drawn their members attention to it. After all, other sports have managed it. But Dave Collins, chairman of the BASES psychology group, says he has never been officially contacted by the Football Association.

Even so it seems that players are finding out for themselves; and many BASES-accredited psychologists admit that they are seeing more and more footballers. Dr Dave Collins for instance: 'I have had around a dozen come to see me in the last two years and I am working with four at present. It is a similar story with my colleagues'.

The problem is that with relatively few accredited sports psychologists to choose from, some players are no doubt falling into the clutches of those practising what Howard Wilkinson describes as 'different disciplines'.

With a paucity of accredited practitioners and such a demand from elsewhere, sport psychologists will continue to thrive even if football continues to give them the cold shoulder. Many make a good living by branching outside sport. Motivational psychologists are widely used throughout industry to help support recruitment and training. The likes of John Sire, Richard Cox and Dave Collins can live without football, but in an environment as competitive as modern football, where the smallest advantage can make the difference between winning and losing, and where it is not just points and prizes at stake but vast sums of cash – can football live without them?

CHAPTER SIXTEEN

When the Shooting Stops
Football in the Fight Against Crime

The first game ever played by Moss Side Amateur Reserves is probably the most notorious football match ever to have taken place in Manchester. It has gained a reputation as the truce match which signalled the beginning of the end of a bloody and murderous gang war. It is the most dramatic example of how soccer is being used all over the country to reduce crime. Some probation services are even prescribing soccer as part of the rehabilitation of serious offenders.

Many of the people who live in Moss Side play down its reputation for drugs and violence. Comparisons with Beirut, made by some newspapers, are certainly over the top, but there is no smoke without fire and in Moss Side it is often the fire of a semi-automatic weapon. A long-running turf war between two drug-dealing gangs earned this part of South Manchester many damning headlines in the 1980s and early 1990s. The gangs took their names from two of the streets in a tightly packed, low-rise 1960s housing estate, the Gooch Close gang and the Dodington Close gang. Incidents included rival members being shot by masked men on mountain bikes, pubs being sprayed with gunfire and children as young as 14 becoming both victims and culprits. Then in 1995 there was a change.

'We were able to achieve a decrease in crime statistics of just under two per cent in a year, which was quite an achievement in an inner-city area at that time,' says Superintendent Lillian King, a senior Police Officer in Moss Side during the most difficult years. From behind her desk on the first floor of a stongly fortified police station, the smart superintendent with short, fair hair and authoritative manner, asks a constable to make the coffee and explains the difference she has seen in the area: 'It has been quite evident to me that there's been a lot of change in the area. It has been quite dramatic and the long-term future for the area is positive.'

There are a number of reasons why crime in Moss Side decreased in 1995, but one important factor was the founding of new football team, Moss Side Amateur Reserves

Throughout 1995 some of the major players in the Moss Side gang culture were being freed from prison. Other men like Howard Swarray had served time for drug dealing following an undercover police investigation called Operation China in 1992. The 'China' court case claimed the Gooch Close gang had more than 50 members and controlled hundreds of drug trades in the alleyways of their estate. Nineteen gang members pleaded guilty to drug dealing.

While these men were locked up, their younger colleagues continued to sell drugs and protect their nefarious trades with violence. But when the main protagonists were released from jail and returned home, they seemed to have a fresh outlook. They wanted a new focus, and football provided it.

Anthony 'Tiny' Smith, who became captain of the team, recalls what happened: 'It was just a bunch of lads playing football. We'd got nothing to do with our days, the sun was shining and we were bored out of our brains. Someone got a ball out and started playing football, and then people got involved. If there were gang members involved then they weren't coming along with the attitude of gang members, it was just football and it was all about enjoying ourselves because we had nothing better to do. I preferred it that way, they were playing football rather than gun toting or drug selling or whatever.'

Moss Side already had a very successful amateur team, one which had produced professional players including Gary Bennet, who made nearly 400 appearances for Sunderland, and Wayne Collins, whose career included spells with Crewe, Sheffield Wednesday and Fulham. One of the older players, full-time youth worker Billy Hughes, decided to form a second team, the Moss Side Amateur Reserves who the newly returned players could turn out for. When word got out that the names on the team sheet included members of the Gooch and Dodington gangs, their first game was attended by more members of the local media than there are at some professional games.

One of the journalists for the *Manchester Evening News* remembers the match as a disorganized affair: 'We were sent to the wrong pitch to start with, along with the opposing team. It was only a few mobile phone calls that ensured the match took place at all. The visiting team hadn't been told that the venue had been changed and we all needed to be guided through Moss Side to a school field where Billy Hughes and his team were waiting.'

The players were persuaded, somewhat reluctantly, to pose for a team photo. Journalists were hurriedly matching the names and faces to crime stories they had covered in the past. 'One player was smoking a large spliff (joint) until just before kick off, he had to hold it behind his back when the photo was taken,' says the experienced local newsman. He remembers the quality of the play, though, as much as anything: 'They were very sharp and skilful, a class above their opponents. It was like an exhibition match'. Against a long established team from Wythenshawe, a large housing estate on the Southern edge of Manchester, Moss Side Amateur Reserves triumphed six-nil.

The photo printed by the *Manchester Evening News* looked at first glance like any other local league side. One row of kneeling players in front of another row of standing players. Ages appeared to range from late teens to late twenties and all were black or mixed race. Most of the men wore cheerful smiles beneath short cropped haircuts. But the photo caused a stir at the youth centre.

Billy Hughes received a phone call from the league secretary: 'He was saying, "What's all this? I'm reading here that all your players are members of the Gooch and Dodington."'. Hughes felt threatened and was angry that his players were not being allowed to escape from their past, he remembers: 'I said, "What are you on about? I work with young people and you know my role in the community and you know my job."'.

Hughes felt insulted that a man who organized Sunday football should try and tell him about working with young people, especially ones with backgrounds like the members of this team.

For the first ten games of the season Moss Side Amateur Reserves had the same referee, the secretary of the Referees Association. It's not clear if this was because other referees were too scared to officiate a team of former gang members, or because the secretary wanted to keep a special eye on his newest, and most notorious team. Either way, the players' reputation had marked them out for close attention from the authorities.

Billy Hughes's team had a remarkable début year: 'I thought we'd do well, but I didn't think we'd do as well as we did,' reflected the manager later. 'We won the league, we won two cups and we went unbeaten all season. I think we dropped one point all season in the league. The lads did themselves proud and I think it's something positive coming out of the area.' But he concedes that the team does have another purpose as well as winning matches. 'I'm not saying it's about curbing their behaviour or anything but we are trying to help them. If they're not doing this on a Saturday then they might get themselves locked up again through something they do on the streets.'

Within a year a number of the team members had gone on trial to professional clubs and two had been offered contracts.

Tiny Smith, who is clearly respected as the fast-talking captain, chips in: 'I'll be honest with you, all of us have most probably got something to do with crime 'cos there's nothing for us here anyway. So someone's going to resort to crime, whether it's petty crime or major. Everyone's been in trouble for something.' Tiny's crime was in 1988 when he got caught up in an armed robbery on a post office in another part of Manchester, 'I got six years for that, and I had to stay in police cells all over the place. I was in Lancaster, Morpeth, Scotland. I was all over the place being moved around. My family couldn't keep track of me so they couldn't come and see me. I had a rough time. The only experience I can give to the younger players is that the jailhouse isn't a nice place, and I've told them that.'

Billy Hughes hopes that the younger members of the team

will learn from the mistakes of their seniors: 'No matter what has happened in the past, we all make mistakes in life and we like to correct them. Football is challenge anyway, it opens doors to different things.'

When Moss Side Amateur Reserves played their first match in full view of the media, Billy is sure the police were watching, too. Superintendent Lillian King knows a fair amount about the team, but if there was any suspicion about the motives of the players at the start, Ms King is now full of praise, 'I think it's great to see that they can set an example, and that they can shout about the benefits as well. Because if the right message is given out by this team to the youngsters of Moss Side then, of course, it will make a difference in the future. If you take a group of young people who find a way to constructively use their time then you begin to notice a change. I can't say all the crime figures have dropped dramatically just because of a football team, because it's only been part of an overall change in the area where young people are turning away from crime and making a much more focused and potentially useful use of their leisure time.'

One of the people tempting young people away from crime and into sport is former world karate champion Geoff Thompson. Tall, powerful and smartly dressed, Geoff is the charismatic persuader behind the Youth Charter for Sport, a Manchester-based charity which uses sport to motivate bored and disillusioned youngsters.

Geoff, along with Billy Hughes, was one of the instigators of the Moss Side Amateur Reserves. Thompson recalls the first meetings he had with the ex-cons who were to form the backbone of the team: 'The aggression I was dealing with made it very difficult. I had to use my karate training to deflect the aggression and potential violence and I had to refocus that energy. Some of these cases were quite extreme in terms of the experiences they had had.'

Even some of the players who had not been arrested for drug dealing or violence themselves had been the victims of the gang war. The team's first centre-forward, Adrian Stapleton, had been shot in the mouth, chest, arms and legs in one 1991 attack. Geoff Thompson says he was shocked by some of the stories he was told: 'I had the innocent idea of going in and saying, "Let's give them some kit and a little encouragement and off they go". I soon found it was a very different ball game.'

But Geoff did see a willingness to change among the players. He says the founding of the team was just a response to the gang members' desire to play football: 'It was the young people who decided not to cancel each other out any more. All I said was that they had to be rewarded when they did something constructive.'

From a safe distance Superintendent King saw the results. 'I think young people who are able to find some discipline and then put in a commitment to sport rather than in to crime will obviously have a brighter future,' she says.

Moss Side Amateur Reserves have not completely changed the area, or its reputation. Indeed one of the players in that first game, Errol Jones, was later convicted of a murder in Bristol. But Moss Side did see a drop in violence, especially shootings, when the team started, and this is only one example of how football is being used to curb crime.

Ricky Otto is a perfect example of a man who used football as an escape route from a life of crime. Six years as a pro with Leyton Orient, Southend and Birmingham City is two years longer than he was sentenced to spend in prison. He says that as a youth he'd steal anything: 'I was into most crimes, you know, burglaries, robberies, frauds, cheque books. Life for me was just walking around the streets with my mates finding a way of making enough money to buy clothes and jewellery and then to drive around in a car like a bad man.'

At his last trial Otto was described by the judge as a bully, a thief and a thug: 'Of my mates, 99.9 per cent are in prison, and I've got mates doing life sentences for murder, so me going to prison was just what was expected.'

Otto says that while he was inside, eight of his friends from school were shot in different East London crimes. He resolved to make the most of his footballing talent and when he came up for parole, his release conditions included compulsory attendance at training sessions with Leyton Orient. At the time it was a radical step for the prison service to allow an inmate to take up such a glamorous exercise routine. But following its success with Ricky and the example of Moss Side Amateur Reserves, prison authorities started to realize that football, as well as other sports, might have something to offer in the rehabilitation of offenders.

In Yorkshire, a number of organizations in the leisure sector are working together with the probation services to make sport part of the conditions for release for offenders. Not just for those, like Ricky Otto, who are good enough to make a career out of sport, but for any offender who they think will benefit from a sporting chance. Norman Abusin is a Leeds probation officer who interviews prisoners towards the end of their sentences to asses them for suitability for a scheme called 'Sporting Chance'. He says all sorts of criminals can be involved: 'They ranges from car thieves and burglars all the way up to people on life sentences for sex offences and murder.'

Mr Abusin is acutely aware of accusations that this is a cushy option for people who ought to be locked up for their crimes rather than given privileges like special access to sports facilities. In the scheme's defence he points out that the Sporting Chance programme comes after, not instead of, punishment. 'You've got to realize that we take these people on face value, they're given a second chance with us. We take their offences into account but at the end of the day they've already been punished and we're working towards their rehabilitation, and we've found that sport can be used in that process.'

Prisoners will to talk to Norman Abusin on the recommendation of the probation service. The Chief Probation Officer in West Yorkshire, David Brereton, says his staff only choose certain types of offenders for the scheme, 'The bulk of the people we refer to Sporting Chance will be those who the officers believe have a considerable risk of re-offending.'

Mark Griffin was one such prisoner. A thin young man with a long, purposeful stride, he is one of the shining examples of the Sporting Chance programme. 'Well, I've been in and out of

jail most of my life, basically for drug-related offences and stealing,' says Griffin who sold drugs as well as developing a £70-
a-day habit himself, 'When I first started it was just speed
and dope, then I got introduced to heroin while I was serving
time in Liverpool Prison. From then on, I was basically in and
out of prison on loads of charges, and then when I came up for
probation they said they'd give me a chance. I'd been on
probation before but it was never as good as this.'

There are many examples of men with similar stories to
Mark in Yorkshire. Norman Abusin says success is measured
simply in terms of whether or not the prisoner ends up in
trouble again. 'Ultimately things can only be monitored on re-
offending rates,' continues the sports counsellor: 'We see clients,
who were never involved in sport, playing actively with friends
and family, their self-confidence increases and they're filling
their time with a constructive activity. We can see that as a
success in itself, but the only way you can measure that success
is if the rates of re-offending fall.'

David Brereton, West Yorkshire's Chief Probation Officer,
agrees: 'We certainly aren't talking about measuring success in
terms of sporting prowess, although for some people that might
be appropriate. It's much more to do with getting the re-
offending rates down, that's why we're in business.'

The use of football as a crime-stopping tool could easily be
dismissed as just another distraction to use up the spare time and
energy of youngsters who would otherwise fall into bad habits,
but these examples are much more than that. Sport has been
systematically measured and found to reach the parts of society
that other well-meaning probation initiatives fail to reach.

Professor Peter Taylor and his team in the University of
Sheffield Leisure Management Unit, were asked by to assess the
results of sports counselling by the organizers of one of the early
pilot schemes in West Yorkshire. 'This was *the* most thorough
investigation of this particular issue that had ever been done,'
enthuses Professor Taylor.

From the very start the idea of using sport in this way fascinated a man more used to analyzing industrial statistics. 'As an

economist I had long been talking about the principle of giving people constructive leisure pursuits as a way of keeping them away from trouble. The idea is easy to trip off the tongue, but no proper evidence had ever been gathered to back it up, so I jumped at the opportunity to do the first proper empirical research,' he says.

Keeping people from falling back into trouble is easy to measure. If rates of re-conviction are lower among criminals who have sport made part of their parole conditions, then it works. It is as simple as that.

The team from Sheffield set about their work with energetic vigour and academic rigour. 'First of all our bottom line was a comparative re-conviction rate study. We tracked people coming off this project and matched them against a control group of people in similar circumstances who had not been given sports counselling, and measured any difference in re-conviction rates. In order to do that properly you have got to built up a case history over a decent period of time, and we decided that we needed two years to see if the results were sustained,' explains Professor Taylor.

The project has never been compulsory. Anyone who hates sport can choose not to take part, but once a prisoner has opted in, they are expected to complete the course. It would be easy for critics to claim that a scheme which only includes people who want to take part is bound to succeed, but the criminals who qualified for sports counselling had long histories of re-offending.

As Professor Taylor explains, these people were the ones the probation service had failed to keep on the straight and narrow. 'If anything, the kind of client profile that we discovered was not the gentle end at all, it was towards the hardened criminal end, definitely the more severe type of offender was being given sports counselling. It was the case of probation officers using sport as a last resort. They had clients they didn't know what to do with and they thought – let's give sports counselling a go.'

Professor Taylor met a number of the people receiving sports counselling. He says some of them were in a mess. 'These are people who shocked me with the unremitting gloom and despair of their lives and this project offered them something positive.'

Despite that fact that the study was centred on what appeared to be the toughened crust of the prison service population, the results were remarkable. Sheffield University's report made some revealing conclusions:

The 23 participants that had completed eight weeks or more of counselling were significantly less likely to re-offend.

The re-conviction rate among offenders involved in sport was 49 per cent compared to an average rate of 63.3 per cent.

Participants were found to gain in self-esteem and physical fitness, leading to a more positive outlook and behaviour.

Professor Taylor's long-held hunch that competitive sport could successfully help redirect criminals towards the legal mainstream had been proved correct, although he concedes that as a probation method, it is expensive. 'The crucial comparison which we weren't commissioned to do, but needs to be done by someone, is to compare the cost- effectiveness of this kind of work against the cost-effectiveness of other treatments for persistent offenders. What we've demonstrated is that this approach, though expensive, does have a beneficial effect.'

Sports Counselling is only available to a small number of repeat offenders in a small section of the country. Elsewhere, in a separate venture, football is being employed to try and guide youngsters before they get into trouble at all...

It is dusk, and an unmarked transit van with lights on the roof slowly crawls along the streets of the Bentilee housing estate in Stoke-on-Trent. Inside the van are specially trained men in uniforms. When this red-brick sprawl was built in the 1960s it was one of the biggest residential developments in Europe. It soon gained a reputation in the locality for being a rough place with high crime levels. The van draws to a halt on a run-down concrete tennis court area, the tall wire perimeter fencing is perforated by gaping holes and the tennis nets are missing.

At the same time as the strong, uniformed young men burst out the back of the van, a hydraulic mast stretches high above the wasteland carrying powerful floodlights connected to a free-standing generator. The staring bulbs-on-a-stick throw light all across the courts, as pockets of youths emerge from the corners. 'All right, Mark?' hails one of the scruffy youngsters to the van's driver, 'I've brought me brother along, can he play as well?'

Mark Roberts drives Stoke City Council's Streetsport van on to Bentilee every Tuesday evening. His colleagues throw open the back doors and unload self-assembly goal posts, balls and cones to mark the edge of the pitch. With the floodlights included, this is not just a van, it's a mobile leisure centre. 'If we didn't come up here there'd be nothing going on because there's no floodlights and no goals,' Says Mark as the youngsters help his colleague put up the portable posts. 'They value what we bring, and we come every week at the same time. We're here, whatever the weather.'

There used to be nets on the tennis courts and goal posts on the grass, but the facilities fell victim to the vandalism and petty crime for which the estate became famous. The local council got tired of replacing equipment only for it to be stolen or destroyed, so the hit-and-run provision offered by the van seemed an ideal solution. Mark Roberts reckons that once people realize they can gain more enjoyment from using the goals than they can from abusing them, then it will be safe to provide permanent facilities, 'I think what we're trying to do is to show that there's a need for sports facilities, and the kids do value them. If we put in proper goals and floodlights now, I think they'd be used instead of smashed up and stuff'.

The locals pick themselves into football teams of around 14 a side. Mark stands back as one of his colleagues referees the match. It's a very informal affair. No matching kits, no yellow cards and no football boots. When the game is over, the goals are packed away, the floodlights are gently lowered to fit snugly on the van's roof and the youth-workers go home. Behind them they leave tired young people still disputing which of them played the best and who was tripped by who. A couple of boys, aged about 14, are quite open about what they'd be doing if the van hadn't turned up: 'We'd just have messed around like we did before. Everybody here would be involved in some sort of trouble, no mistake.'

Streetsport is the idea of Kevin Sauntry, a sizeable, athletic figure who almost fills his box-room office on his own. It was as an independent youth-worker that he had the idea of bussing sports facilities into rough areas to try to reduce crime. Then the council bought into the project and made Kevin its head. Explaining what the aims are, he says, 'It's got nothing to do with character building, in the sense of rigid, disciplined activities with adults barking instructions at young people who all have short hair and jump up and down in lines. It's got to do with sport meaning something to a community and bringing adults and young people together in the same activity. Sport, especially football, is something that is shared by all ages, so why not use it as a positive force for young people?'.

Mr Sauntry claims crime figures for the area have fallen since his project has been taking pitches to the people. He says police officers tell him of the difference his simple venture has made to the levels of violence in the area. Kevin himself says the best measure of success is less easy to quantify: 'When you get less complaints from people who live in the neighbourhood – complaints about anything – when you go on to an estate and see young people and adults relating to each other rather than standing in separate groups on street corners, and when you see young people turn their backs on drug-pushers so they can come and play football, as I have seen and it has gladdened my heart, then it's got to be a success'.

A similarly encouraging story of sport being used to cut crime can be found in Huddersfield. David Morby, a council recreation officer and one of the first people to use sports counselling, established a scheme in schools in the rougher parts of the town. He says it was initially only a pilot scheme: 'The twilight activity scheme was piloted on four school areas,' explains Mr Morby. 'The areas were picked for various reasons, but one thing they all had in common was a problem of vandalism, especially to the school buildings and grounds.'

The twilight scheme took sport into the school grounds two nights week for five hours. After 16 weeks, the benefits were clear to see, as Mr Morby recalls, 'At the end of the scheme, the local residents indicated that things had improved dramatically during the period of operation. Notably, the financial analysis showed that the schools would normally have anticipated a very large claim on insurance for vandalism, and when the figures were compared with the previous year, there was a considerable saving'. Clearly it had been shown again that football was turning people away from crime.

With such conclusive evidence coming from such a wide range of sources, one might expect the Home Office to be funding the use of soccer to fight crime. But, despite the success of informal football alliances made by ex-gang members going straight, formal contracts with prisoners on parole and council provision of facilities for those yet to become criminals, successive governments have been unmoved, choosing instead to give short, sharp, shocks and boot-camps.

The Moss Side Amateur Reserves even saw the youth centre where they were based knocked down. They have no pitch of their own and are involved in a constant struggle for funds. Despite these constraints, the team thrives. In the year that Manchester United won the League, F.A. Cup and Champions League treble, Moss Side Amateurs landed an equally unprecedented treble of their league and both cup competitions. Billy Hughes, who continues to manage them has been awarded with the MBE in recognition of his work with the Moss Side youngsters. Geoff Thompson, one of the catalysts behind the Moss Side team, says it is time that there was a co-ordinated approach from the people who know what sport can achieve, 'The left arm doesn't know what the right arm is doing. Sport is *the* social force for change and if we use it to reach the youth and keep them out of trouble then it's win, win for everyone.'

INDEX